Barbecue

Published in 2011 by Murdoch Books Pty Limited.

Murdoch Books Pty Ltd
Pier 8/9, 23 Hickson Road,
Millers Point NSW 2000
Phone: + 61 (0) 2 8220 2000
Fax: + 61 (0) 2 8220 2558
www.murdochbooks.com.au

Murdoch Books UK Limited
Erico House, 6th Floor
93–99 Upper Richmond Road
Putney, London SW15 2TG
Phone: +44 (0)20 8785 5995
Fax: +44 (0)20 8785 5985
www.murdochbooks.co.uk

Publisher: Lynn Lewis
Project Manager: Liz Malcolm
Designer: Kylie Mulquin
Editor: Zoe Harpham
Production: Alexandra Gonzalez

National Library of Australia Cataloguing-in-Publication:
Title: Barbecue.
ISBN: 978-1-74266-508-5 (pbk.)
Series: Easy eats.
Notes: Includes index.
Subjects: Barbecuing. Cooking.
Dewey Number. 641.578

Printed by Hang Tai Printing Company Limited, China.
PRINTED IN CHINA

IMPORTANT: Those who might be at risk from the effects of salmonella poisoning (the elderly, pregnant women, young children and
those suffering from immune deficiency diseases) should consult their doctor with any concerns about eating raw eggs.

CONVERSION GUIDE: You may find cooking times vary depending on the oven you are using.
For fan-forced ovens, as a general rule, set the oven temperature to 20°C (35°F) lower than indicated in the recipe.

Barbecue

more than 100 recipes for outdoor cooking

MURDOCH BOOKS

Contents

Meat

Delicious marinades transform steaks, kebabs, chicken and sausages into special barbecue fare.

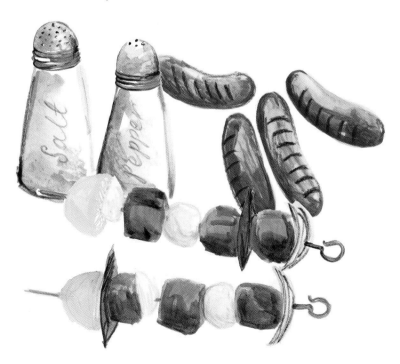

YOGHURT CHICKEN WITH INDIAN SPICES

preparation time 20 minutes plus at least 20 minutes marinating
cooking time 20 minutes
serves 4

4 chicken breast fillets
1 tablespoon ground cumin
1 tablespoon freshly ground black
   pepper
2 teaspoons ground cinnamon
2 teaspoons turmeric
4 garlic cloves, crushed
2 tablespoons grated fresh ginger

330 g (11½ oz/1¼ cups) Greek-style
   yoghurt
2 tablespoons olive oil
4 tomatoes, cut into wedges
1 cup mint
2 small red onions, thinly sliced
2 tablespoons lemon juice
sweet mango chutney and naan
   bread, to serve

● Place the chicken fillets on a board. Working with one fillet at a time, use a large sharp knife and with one hand on top of the fillet to steady it, cut through the middle horizontally to butterfly the fillet; take care not to cut the fillet all the way through. Open the fillet up. Repeat with the remaining fillets.

● Heat a non-stick frying pan over a medium–high heat. Add the spices to the pan and cook, stirring, for 1 minute or until fragrant. Transfer the mixture to a bowl. Add the garlic, ginger and yoghurt to the spice mixture in the bowl, add the chicken and toss to coat in the mixture. Cover with plastic wrap, then refrigerate for at least 20 minutes and up to 8 hours.

● Drain the chicken well. Preheat a barbecue hotplate or chargrill pan to high direct heat, then brush with the oil. Add the chicken in batches and cook for 4 minutes on each side, or until golden and cooked through. Season to taste

● Combine the tomato, mint, onion and lemon juice in a small bowl. Place the chicken and tomato salad on a plate and serve with chutney and naan.

CHARGRILLED PIRI-PIRI SPATCHCOCK

preparation time 20 minutes plus at least 4 hours marinating
cooking time 20 minutes
serves 4

2 tablespoons chilli flakes or to taste, roasted
8 garlic cloves or to taste, crushed
4 tablespoons paprika
250 ml (9 fl oz/1 cup) lemon juice
1 tablespoon red wine vinegar

310 ml (11 fl oz/1¼ cups) olive oil, plus extra, for cooking
1 bunch coriander (cilantro) leaves, chopped
4 spatchcocks
4 lemons, halved

● Place the chilli flakes, garlic, paprika, lemon juice, vinegar and olive oil in a bowl and stir to combine well. Stir in the coriander.

● Rinse the spatchcocks, then pat dry with paper towels. Place the spatchcocks, breast side down, on a board. Working with one spatchcock at a time, use a pair of sharp kitchen scissors to cut down both sides of the backbone, then discard the bone. Open the spatchcock up, flattening it with the heel of your hand. Place it in a bowl, spoon half the marinade over, then rub it in well. Cover and refrigerate for 4 hours or overnight.

● Preheat a barbecue hotplate or chargrill pan to medium–low direct heat. Drain the spatchcocks well, reserving the marinade, then brush with the extra oil and cook, skin side down, for 20 minutes, brushing occasionally with the reserved marinade. Turn the spatchcocks, then cover with the barbecue lid or foil and cook, brushing occasionally with the marinade, for another 15–20 minutes, or until cooked through and the skin is well charred. While the spatchcocks are cooking, place the lemons, cut side down, onto the barbecue, and cook for 3 minutes.

Meat

CHICKEN SATAY WITH PEANUT SAUCE AND BOK CHOY

preparation time 20 minutes plus 1–2 hours marinating
cooking time 20 minutes
serves 4

2 teaspoons mild curry powder
2 garlic cloves, crushed
1 teaspoon finely grated fresh ginger
125 ml (4 fl oz/½ cup) coconut milk
600 g (1 lb 5 oz) chicken thighs fillets, trimmed and cut into 1 cm (½ inch) pieces
vegetable oil, for brushing
3 baby bok choy (pak choy), leaves separated
steamed jasmine rice, to serve

PEANUT SAUCE
1 teaspoon peanut oil
2 garlic cloves, finely chopped
2 red Asian shallots, finely chopped
125 g (4½ oz/½ cup) crunchy peanut butter
1 tablespoon fish sauce
1 tablespoon lime juice
1 teaspoon soft brown sugar
125 ml (4 fl oz/½ cup) coconut milk

• Put the curry powder, garlic, ginger and coconut milk in a bowl and stir to combine well. Add the chicken, toss to coat all over, then cover and refrigerate for 1–2 hours.

• Meanwhile, soak 12 wooden skewers in cold water for 30 minutes to prevent scorching.

• Meanwhile, make the peanut sauce. Heat the peanut oil in a small saucepan over medium heat. Add the garlic and shallot and sauté for 1 minute, then stir in the peanut butter, fish sauce, lime juice, sugar and coconut milk and 125 ml (4 fl oz/½ cup) water. Cook, stirring, for 3–5 minutes, or until well combined. Keep warm until required; if the oil starts to separate out, stir in a little more water until combined.

- Preheat a barbecue hotplate or large, heavy-based frying pan to high direct heat, then brush with a little oil. Thread the chicken onto the skewers, making sure the pieces are not too tightly pressed together. Cook the chicken skewers for 3–4 minutes on each side, or until the chicken is golden and cooked.

- Meanwhile, cook the bok choy in a saucepan of salted water for 2–3 minutes, or until just wilted. Drain well, then chop.

- Serve the skewers immediately with the bok choy and the satay sauce for drizzling over, with a bowl of steamed jasmine rice to the side.

CAJUN CHICKEN WITH CORN FRITTERS AND A TANGY TOMATO RELISH

preparation time 20 minutes
cooking time 45 minutes
serves 6

vegetable oil, for cooking
6 chicken thighs fillets (about 500 g/
   1 lb 2 oz in total), trimmed, then
   cut in half lengthways
1 tablespoon cajun seasoning
1 lime, cut into wedges

TANGY TOMATO RELISH

1 tablespoon olive oil
1 small red onion, finely chopped
1 garlic clove, crushed
1 teaspoon finely grated fresh ginger
400 g (14 oz) tin chopped tomatoes
1 tablespoon soft brown sugar
2 tablespoons fresh lime juice

CORN FRITTERS

110 g (4 oz/¾ cup) plain
   (all-purpose) flour
½ teaspoon bicarbonate of soda
   (baking soda)
½ teaspoon paprika
2 eggs, lightly beaten
125 ml (4 fl oz/½ cup) milk
300 g (10½ oz/2 cups) frozen corn
   kernels, thawed and drained well
2 spring onions (scallions), finely sliced
2 tablespoons chopped coriander
   (cilantro) leaves
2 teaspoons finely chopped red chilli

• To make the tangy tomato relish, heat the olive oil in a small frying pan over medium heat and sauté the onion, garlic and ginger for 5 minutes, or until softened. Add the tomatoes, sugar and lime juice and cook over low heat for 30 minutes, or until the sauce is thick and slightly jammy.

• Meanwhile, make the corn fritters. Sift the flour, bicarbonate of soda and paprika into a bowl and season well with sea salt and freshly ground black pepper. In a small bowl, whisk the eggs and milk until combined, then add to the flour mixture and whisk to a smooth batter. Stir in the corn and spring onion, then cover and leave to stand for 10 minutes.

• Preheat a barbecue hotplate or non-stick frying pan to medium direct heat. Brush with 1 tablespoon of oil. Working in batches, spoon 2 tablespoons of batter per fritter onto the hotplate, spreading it if necessary to form rounds (you should end up with about 12 fritters). Cook for 2–3 minutes on each side, or until golden and cooked through, adding extra oil as needed. Cover the fritters and keep warm.

• Coat the chicken pieces with the cajun seasoning and some sea salt and freshly ground black pepper, then brush with oil.

• Heat the barbecue hotplate or heavy-based frying pan to high direct heat and brush with oil. Cook the chicken pieces for 4 minutes on each side, or until cooked through and golden.

• Divide the corn fritters among plates and top with the chicken. Stir the coriander and chilli through the tomato relish and spoon over the chicken. Serve with lime wedges.

Meat

CHICKEN, BACON AND AVOCADO BURGER WITH MUSTARD MAYO

preparation time 15 minutes
cooking time 15 minutes
serves 6

750 g (1 lb 10 oz) minced (ground)
   chicken
2 spring onions (scallions), finely sliced
125 g (4½ oz/1½ cups) fresh
   breadcrumbs
1 egg, lightly beaten
2 tablespoons chopped flat-leaf
   (Italian) parsley
1 tablespoon olive oil
6 slices of bacon, cut in half
6 hamburger buns

butter lettuce leaves, to serve
2 tomatoes, sliced
1 large avocado, sliced

MUSTARD MAYO
125 g (4 oz/½ cup) whole-egg
   mayonnaise
3 teaspoons lemon juice
1 tablespoon wholegrain mustard,
   or to taste

● Put the chicken, spring onion, breadcrumbs, egg and parsley in a bowl and
season with sea salt and freshly ground black pepper. Using clean hands, mix
until well combined, then divide into six even portions. Using damp hands, form
each into a 12 cm (4½ inch) round, then flatten slightly to form patties.

● Preheat a barbecue hotplate or large frying pan to medium direct heat. Cook
the patties in two batches for 4 minutes on each side, or until golden and
cooked through. Drain on paper towels, then transfer to a plate and cover with
foil to keep warm.

● Wipe the hotplate clean, then cook the bacon for 3 minutes on each side, or until crisp. Drain on paper towels.

● Meanwhile, preheat the grill (broiler) to medium. Slice the hamburger buns in half through the middle, place on a baking tray and toast under the grill on both sides until golden.

● In a bowl, mix together the mustard mayo ingredients. Transfer the hamburger bases to plates, then top each with some lettuce leaves, a pattie, some tomato, bacon and avocado. Spoon some mustard mayo over the burgers before putting the lids on top.

Meat

TURKISH STEAK SANDWICH WITH RED ONION JAM

preparation time 15 minutes

cooking time 35 minutes

serves 4

olive oil, for brushing

1 loaf of Turkish bread, cut into
    4 even portions

4 x 80–100 g (3–3½ oz) pieces of
    minute (thin) steak, pounded thinly
    using a meat mallet

hummus, to serve

225 g (8 oz) tin sliced beetroot
    (beets), drained

3 large tomatoes, sliced

1 large handful of shredded iceberg
    lettuce

mayonnaise, to drizzle

RED ONION JAM

1 tablespoon olive oil

1 large red onion, halved and
    finely sliced

1 garlic clove, finely chopped

1 tablespoon soft brown sugar

1 tablespoon balsamic vinegar

4 Japanese (slender) eggplants
    (aubergines), cut into slices 5 mm
    (¼ inch) thick

3 zucchini (courgettes), cut
    lengthways into slices 5 mm
    (¼ inch) thick

- To make the red onion jam, heat the olive oil in a saucepan, add the onion and garlic and cook over low heat, stirring often, for 10–12 minutes, or until the onion is very soft and deep golden. Add the sugar, vinegar and 2 tablespoons water and cook for a further 10–12 minutes, or until thick and jammy.

- Meanwhile, preheat a barbecue hotplate or large frying pan to medium direct heat. Lightly brush the eggplant and zucchini slices with olive oil, then cook in batches for 2–3 minutes on each side, or until tender. Set aside in a bowl.

- Cut the Turkish bread into four even portions, then slice each in half lengthways. Cook on the barbecue or a chargrill pan until crispy. Alternatively, cook under a grill (broiler) for 1–2 minutes.

- Lightly brush the steaks with olive oil and barbecue over medium heat for 1–2 minutes on each side, or until done to your liking.

- Spread half the Turkish bread bases with hummus, then add the beetroot, eggplant and zucchini. Top with the steak, tomato slices and some lettuce, then drizzle with mayonnaise. Place the other bread slices on top and cut each sandwich in half. Serve with the onion jam.

Meat

MARINATED STEAK WITH RED RICE AND BEANS

preparation time 20 minutes plus overnight marinating and 10 minutes resting
cooking time 30 minutes
serves 4

800 g (1 lb 12 oz) piece of skirt steak
  (about 1 cm/½ inch thick), trimmed
  of all sinew
1 bunch (150 g/5½ oz) flat-leaf
  (Italian) parsley, leaves picked
1 tablespoon dried oregano
3 tablespoons red wine vinegar
125 ml (4 fl oz/½ cup) olive oil,
  plus extra, for pan-frying
4 garlic cloves, chopped

RED RICE AND BEANS
3 tablespoons olive oil
1 small onion, finely chopped
200 g (7 oz/1 cup) long-grain white
  rice
375 ml (13 fl oz/1½ cups) chicken
  stock
3 tablespoons tomato paste
  (concentrated purée)
400 g (14 oz) tin red kidney beans,
  rinsed and drained
chopped coriander (cilantro) leaves,
  to serve

- Lay the steak in a glass or ceramic dish. Put the parsley, oregano, vinegar, olive oil and garlic in a food processor with some sea salt and freshly ground black pepper. Process until a coarse paste forms, then pour the mixture over the steak and rub it in well on both sides. Cover and refrigerate overnight.

- To prepare the red rice and beans, heat the olive oil in a saucepan over medium heat, then sauté the onion for 5 minutes, or until softened. Add the rice, stock and tomato paste and bring to the boil. Reduce the heat to medium−low, then cover and cook on low heat for 15−20 minutes, or until the rice is tender, adding a little more water if necessary. Remove from the heat and stir in the kidney beans. Cover and leave to stand for 5 minutes, then fluff up the grains with a fork.

- Meanwhile, preheat a barbecue hotplate or heavy-based frying pan to medium−high direct heat. Drain the steak well, then pat with paper towels to remove the excess liquid, taking care not to remove any of the herb coating. Brush with oil, then cook the steak for 1−1 ½ minutes on each side, or until well browned but still a little rare in the middle — take care not to overcook the steak or it will be tough. Transfer to a plate, cover loosely with foil and leave to rest in a warm place for 10 minutes.

- Slice the beef into thin strips and serve with the rice sprinkled with coriander.

Meat

CUMIN AND CINNAMON-DUSTED STEAK

preparation time 20 minutes plus 15 minutes marinating
cooking time 15 minutes
serves 4

6 x 150 g (5½ oz) sirloin or rump
   steaks, each about 2 cm (¾ inch)
   thick
2 tablespoons olive oil, plus extra,
   for brushing
½ teaspoon ground cinnamon
1 teaspoon ground cumin
¼ teaspoon sweet paprika
1 teaspoon sea salt

2 onions, thinly sliced
2 red capsicums (peppers), thinly
   sliced
1–2 red chillies, finely chopped
1 garlic clove, finely chopped
1 tablespoon small oregano leaves
baked potatoes, to serve
sour cream, to serve
dijon mustard, to serve

● Brush both sides of each steak with olive oil. In a small bowl, mix together
the spices and sea salt and dust evenly over each side of each steak. Cover and
set aside for 15 minutes.

● Heat the olive oil in a heavy-based frying pan over medium heat. Add the
onion and sauté for 5 minutes, or until softened. Add the capsicum, chilli, garlic
and oregano and cook for 5–8 minutes, or until the capsicum is well softened,
stirring occasionally.

● Meanwhile, preheat a barbecue hotplate or chargrill pan to high direct heat.
Brush the steaks all over with more olive oil, then cook for 3 minutes on each
side for medium, or until done to your liking. Remove to a warmed plate, cover
loosely with foil and leave to rest for 5 minutes.

● Divide the steaks among serving plates and top with the capsicum mixture.
Serve with baked potatoes topped with a dollop of sour cream, and some
dijon mustard on the side.

SCOTCH FILLET WITH ANCHOVY BUTTER

preparation time 20 minutes plus 1 hour refrigeration
cooking time 10 minutes
serves 4

4 x 175 g (6 oz) Scotch fillet steaks
Olive oil, for brushing steaks
150 g (5½ oz) baby butterbeans (lima
    beans), trimmed
150 g (5½ oz) baby green beans

ANCHOVY BUTTER
4 anchovy fillets
75 g (3 oz) unsalted butter, softened
1 teaspoon finely chopped rosemary
1 garlic clove, crushed
1 teaspoon finely grated lemon rind
    (optional)

- For the anchovy butter, chop the anchovy fillets very finely until you have a mashed consistency. Combine the butter, anchovies, rosemary, garlic and lemon, if using, in a small bowl. Mix well with a fork and season with freshly ground black pepper. Spoon the butter along the middle of a 30 x 15 cm (12 x 6 inch) piece of baking paper. Form into a log shape, about 3 cm (1¼ inches) in diameter, then roll paper around the butter to enclose completely. Carefully transfer the butter to a tray and refrigerate for at least 1 hour or until set. Anchovy butter can be made up to 1 week in advance.

- Preheat a barbecue chargrill plate or large, heavy-based frying pan to high direct heat. Lightly oil the steaks on each side and season with sea salt and freshly ground black pepper. Cook the steaks for 3–4 minutes each side for medium-rare, or until cooked to your liking. Transfer to a plate and cover loosely with foil.

- Meanwhile, cook the beans in a large saucepan of boiling salted water for 5–7 minutes until just tender. Drain well. Cut the anchovy butter into 1 cm (½ inch) thick slices. Divide the beans and steaks among serving plates, top steaks with discs of butter and serve immediately.

Meat

STEAK WITH SPICED BRAISED CARROTS

preparation time 20 minutes
cooking time 1 hour 20 minutes
serves 6

2 tablespoons olive oil

2 red onions, cut into wedges

2 teaspoons ground cumin

2 teaspoons fennel seeds

1 teaspoon ground turmeric

a large pinch of saffron threads

2 tablespoons honey

3 wide orange zest strips

1.5 kg (3 lb 5 oz) carrots, quartered
lengthways

250 ml (9 fl oz/1 cup) chicken stock

3 tablespoons orange juice

155 g (5½ oz/1 cup) pitted green
olives

6 x 150 g (5½ oz) skirt or minute
steaks

100 g (3½ oz) baby green beans,
trimmed

1 small handful coriander (cilantro)
leaves, chopped

45 g (1½ oz/½ cup) toasted flaked
almonds

- Preheat the covered barbecue or oven to 180°C (350°F/Gas 4).

- Heat half the olive oil in a large flameproof baking dish over medium–high heat. Add the onion and sauté for 5 minutes, or until browned lightly. Add the spices and cook, stirring, for 1 minute, or until fragrant.

- Add the honey, orange zest strips and carrots and stir to coat the carrots in the spices. Pour in the stock, orange juice and 125 ml (4 fl oz/½ cup) water and bring to the boil.

- Cover the dish tightly with foil and bake for 40 minutes. Remove the foil and bake for another 30 minutes, or until the carrots are tender. Stir in the olives.

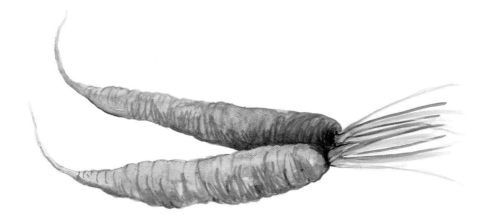

• Just before serving, preheat a barbecue hotplate or large frying pan to medium–high direct heat. Brush with oil, add the steaks and cook for 1–2 minutes on each side, or until done to your liking. Transfer to a plate and cover with foil to keep warm.

• Meanwhile, cook the beans in a small saucepan of boiling salted water for 3 minutes, or until tender. Drain well.

• Divide the steaks, braised carrots and beans among serving plates. Serve sprinkled with the coriander and flaked almonds.

VEAL CUTLETS WITH PARSNIP MASH AND FIG SALAD

preparation time 20 minutes
cooking time 25 minutes
serves 4

8 parsnips, peeled, cored and sliced
500 ml (17 fl oz/2 cups) vegetable
   stock
20–40 g (¾ –1½ oz) melted butter
4 handfuls rocket (arugula)
8 dried figs, thinly sliced
115 g (4 oz/1 cup) toasted walnut
   halves, chopped
2 tablespoons olive oil
4 x 200 g (7 oz) veal cutlets, about
   1 cm (½ inch) thick

CHARDONNAY SAUCE
4 small French shallots, finely
   chopped
250 ml (9 fl oz/1 cup) chardonnay
500 ml (17 fl oz/2 cups) cream
40 g (1½ oz) butter, chopped

● Place the parsnips in a small saucepan over medium heat, add the vegetable stock and bring to the boil. Cook for 15 minutes or until soft. Drain the parsnip, reserving the cooking liquid. Measure 3–4 tablespoons of the liquid and combine with the parsnips and butter in a food processor, discarding the remaining liquid. Process until smooth, then season to taste with sea salt and freshly ground black pepper. Keep warm.

● For the salad, combine the rocket, figs, walnuts and oil in a small bowl and toss to combine well. Set aside.

● Preheat a barbecue hotplate or frying pan to medium–high direct heat, add the veal and cook 3 minutes on each side or until cooked through but still a little pink in the middle. Remove to a plate, cover with foil and keep warm.

● To make the chardonnay sauce, place the shallot and wine in a saucepan over medium–low heat. Bring to the boil, reduce the heat to low and cook for a few minutes or until reduced by half. Add the cream, increase the heat to medium, bring to the boil, then reduce the heat to low and cook for 3–4 minutes or until reduced by half. Whisk in the butter.

● To serve place a large spoonful of the parsnip mash on the plate, place the cutlet to one side of the mash, then spoon the sauce over. Place the salad on the side and serve immediately.

CURRIED LAMB SKEWERS WITH ROCKET, TOMATO AND CORIANDER SALAD

preparation time 20 minutes plus 30 minutes refrigeration
cooking time 15 minutes
serves 8

1 kg (2 lb 4 oz) minced (ground) lamb
1 onion, finely chopped
2 long green chillies, finely chopped
3 garlic cloves, crushed
4 tablespoons korma curry paste
65 g (2¼ oz/½ cup) pistachio nuts,
   finely chopped
2 tablespoons chopped flat-leaf
   (Italian) parsley, plus extra, to
   garnish
lemon wedges, to serve
olive oil, for brushing

CUMIN-SPICED ONION
1 tablespoon cumin seeds
40 g (1½ oz) butter
4 onions, thinly sliced

**ROCKET, TOMATO AND
   CORIANDER SALAD**
150 g (5½ oz) rocket (arugula)
250 g (9 oz) cherry tomatoes, halved
2 Lebanese (short) cucumbers,
   thinly sliced
1 large handful coriander (cilantro)
   leaves
3 tablespoons lemon juice
100 ml (3½ fl oz) olive oil

• Place the lamb in a large bowl with the onion, chilli, garlic, curry paste, pistachios and parsley. Season with sea salt and freshly ground black pepper and mix well.

• Shape the lamb mixture into 16 patties. Mould each portion around a metal skewer to make a 7.5 cm (3 inch) sausage shape. Refrigerate for 30 minutes to firm slightly.

● To make the cumin-spiced onion, heat a non-stick frying pan over medium–low heat, add the cumin seeds and dry-fry for 2 minutes, or until fragrant, shaking the pan often. Tip the cumin seeds onto a plate.

● Melt the butter in the pan over medium heat, then add the onion and sauté for 10 minutes, or until light golden. Add the cumin seeds, stir well to combine, then cook for another 2 minutes, or until fragrant.

● Meanwhile, preheat a barbecue hotplate or chargrill pan to high direct heat. Brush the lamb skewers with olive oil, add to the hotplate and cook for 8 minutes, or until deep golden and cooked through, turning often.

● In a bowl, toss together the rocket, tomato and coriander salad ingredients. Sprinkle the lamb skewers with extra parsley and serve with the cumin-spiced onion and salad.

Meat

HARISSA LAMB CHOPS WITH APRICOT-PISTACHIO COUSCOUS

preparation time 20 minutes
cooking time 20 minutes
serves 4

1 x 425 g (15 oz) tin apricot halves in
    juice
finely grated rind and juice of
    1 orange
30 g (1 oz) butter
2 tablespoons olive oil
4 tablespoons currants
300 g (10½ oz/1½ cups) instant
    couscous
8 (about 800 g/1 lb 12 oz) lamb loin
    chops
4 tablespoons pistachios, chopped
1 large handful coriander (cilantro)
    leaves, chopped

2 baby cos (romaine) lettuces, washed
    and leaves separated, to serve
    (optional)
lemon wedges, to serve (optional)

HARISSA
2 red capsicums (peppers)
2 teaspoons ground cumin
2 teaspoons ground coriander
1 tablespoon lemon juice, or to taste
2 garlic cloves, chopped
1 teaspoon chilli flakes, or to taste
125 ml (4 fl oz/½ cup) extra virgin
    olive oil

- To make the harissa, preheat the barbecue hotplate to high direct heat. Place the whole capsicums on the hotplate and cook, turning often until the skin is black and blistered all over. Place the capsicums in a plastic bag and seal. When cool enough to handle, remove the blistered skin, stem and seeds. Chop the capsicum flesh coarsely, then combine in a food processor with all the ingredients except the olive oil. Process until a coarse paste forms, then add the olive oil and process until smooth. Season to taste with sea salt and freshly ground black pepper and add a little more lemon juice if necessary.

- Drain the apricots well, reserving the juice. Combine the reserved juice, orange rind and juice, then add enough water to make up to 375 ml (13 fl oz/1 $\frac{1}{2}$ cups). Combine the mixture in a saucepan with the butter and 1 tablespoon of the oil and bring just to the boil.

- Place the currants and couscous in a large heatproof bowl, then pour the hot liquid over the top. Stir to combine, then cover the bowl with plastic wrap and stand for 5 minutes or until liquid is absorbed. Chop the apricots and set aside. Fluff the couscous with a fork.

- Brush the barbecue hotplate with the remaining oil, add the lamb chops and cook over medium heat for 3 minutes on each side or until golden and just cooked through. Transfer to a plate, cover with foil and keep warm. Add the pistachios, apricots and coriander to the couscous. Season to taste.

- Divide the couscous evenly among plates. Place 2 lamb chops on each plate and top with harissa. Serve with cos lettuce leaves and lemon wedges, if using.

Meat

CHARGRILLED LAMB CUTLETS WITH RATATOUILLE AND PESTO

preparation time 20 minutes

cooking time 45 minutes

serves 4–6

1 eggplant (aubergine), cut into 3 cm
(1¼ inch) chunks

1½ teaspoons dried oregano

3 tablespoons olive oil,
plus extra, for brushing

1 red onion, sliced

2 garlic cloves, crushed

2 zucchini (courgettes), cut into 1 cm
(½ inch) rounds

1 red capsicum (pepper), cut into
3 cm (1¼ inch) chunks

400 g (14 oz) tin whole tomatoes

2 teaspoons finely chopped lemon
thyme

1 dried bay leaf

12 French-trimmed lamb cutlets

crusty bread, to serve

PESTO

3 large handfuls basil leaves

1 garlic clove

3 tablespoons pine nuts

50 g (1¾ oz/½ cup) grated parmesan

185 ml (6 fl oz/¾ cup) olive oil, plus
extra, for covering the pesto

● To make the pesto, place the basil, garlic, pine nuts and parmesan in a food processor and blend until finely chopped. With the motor running, gradually add the olive oil in a thin steady stream until smooth, then season to taste with sea salt and freshly ground black pepper. Transfer to a clean container and cover the surface of the pesto with a drizzle of olive oil to stop the pesto discolouring. Refrigerate until required; the pesto will keep for up to 3 days.

● Preheat a covered barbecue or oven to 200°C (400°F/Gas 6) indirect heat. Line a baking tray with a sheet of baking paper.

• Place the eggplant and oregano in a bowl. Drizzle with 2 tablespoons of the olive oil and toss to coat. Spread the eggplant on the baking tray in a single layer and bake for 20 minutes, or until golden.

• Heat the remaining oil in a large heavy-based saucepan over medium heat. Add the onion and garlic and sauté for 3–4 minutes, or until the onion is starting to soften. Add the zucchini, capsicum, tomatoes, thyme, bay leaf, eggplant and 125 ml (4 fl oz/½ cup) water. Bring to the boil, then reduce the heat to medium–low, cover and simmer for 20 minutes, or until the vegetables are soft and tender.

• Meanwhile, preheat a barbecue hotplate or chargrill pan to medium direct heat. Cook the lamb cutlets, in batches if necessary, for 3 minutes on each side, or until just cooked through.

• Divide the ratatouille among serving plates, then top with the lamb cutlets and a dollop of pesto. Serve with crusty bread. Keep any unused ratatouille in an airtight container in the refrigerator for up to 2 days.

Meat

LAMB RUMP WITH CHICKPEA TABOULEH AND CHILLI-YOGHURT SAUCE

preparation time 20 minutes

cooking time 5 minutes

serves 4

700 g (1 lb 9 oz) lamb rump steaks

1 tablespoon olive oil

1 teaspoon ground cumin

90 g (3 oz/½ cup) fine burghul
(cracked wheat)

1 x 400 g (14 oz) tin chickpeas
(garbanzo beans), drained well

2 tomatoes (about 150 g/5½ oz
each), cut into 2 cm (¾ inch) pieces

2 spring onions (scallions), trimmed
and finely sliced

1 handful mint, roughly chopped

1 teaspoon finely grated lemon rind

50 ml (2 fl oz) lemon juice

1 large handful flat-leaf (Italian)
parsley, roughly chopped

1 large handful coriander (cilantro)
leaves, roughly chopped

CHILLI-YOGHURT SAUCE

125 g (4½ oz/½ cup) natural yoghurt

1 long green chilli, or to taste, seeded
and finely chopped

1 tablespoon mint sauce

1 large handful mint, chopped

1 large handful coriander (cilantro)
leaves, chopped

- Preheat the oven to 200°C (400°F/Gas 6).

- Preheat a barbecue hotplate or chargrill pan to medium direct heat. Brush the steaks with half of the olive oil, then sprinkle with the ground cumin and season with sea salt and freshly ground black pepper to taste. Add the lamb steaks and cook for 2 minutes each side for medium-rare or until cooked to your liking. Remove from the heat and place on a plate, loosely cover with foil, then rest in a warm place.

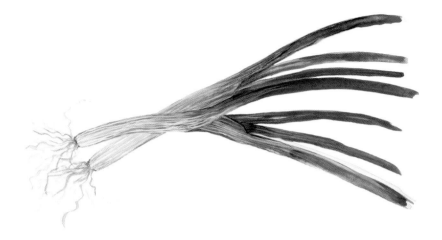

● Place burghul in a bowl. Pour over 375 ml (13 fl oz/1 ½ cups) boiling water, cover and stand for 15 minutes or until tender. Drain well. Stir in the chickpeas, tomato, spring onion, mint, lemon rind and juice, parsley, coriander and remaining olive oil. Season to taste.

● To make the chilli-yoghurt sauce, combine the yoghurt, chilli, mint sauce, mint and coriander in a bowl and stir until smooth.

● Divide the chickpea tabouleh among plates. Slice the lamb steaks thickly on the diagonal, then divide the lamb among serving plates, top with yoghurt sauce and serve immediately.

MOROCCAN LAMB SKEWERS WITH COUSCOUS

preparation time 20 minutes plus 30 minutes marinating
cooking time 10 minutes
serves 4

800 g (1 lb 12 oz) lamb backstraps
    or loin fillets, cut into 3 cm
    (1¼ inch) chunks
6 zucchini (courgettes), sliced
    lengthways about 3 mm (⅛ inch)
    thick
1 tablespoon extra virgin olive oil
375 ml (13 fl oz/1½ cups) chicken
    stock
40 g (1½ oz) butter
250 g (9 oz/1⅓ cups) instant
    couscous
1 teaspoon finely grated lemon rind

1½ tablespoons lemon juice
½ red onion, finely diced
1 large handful coriander (cilantro)
    leaves, plus extra, to garnish

MOROCCAN MARINADE

1 tablespoon Moroccan spice mix
    (available in supermarkets)
2 garlic cloves, crushed
1 teaspoon sea salt flakes
1 teaspoon finely grated lemon rind
1½ tablespoons lemon juice
1 tablespoon extra virgin olive oil

• Soak 8 wooden skewers in cold water for 30 minutes to prevent scorching. Meanwhile, in a small bowl, mix together the Moroccan marinade ingredients. Place the lamb in a bowl, add the marinade and toss to coat, rubbing the mixture in well; cover and marinate in the refrigerator while the skewers soak.

• In a bowl, toss the zucchini slices with the olive oil and season well with sea salt and freshly ground black pepper. Set aside.

- In a saucepan, bring the stock to the boil. Remove from the heat, add the butter and stir until melted. Place the couscous in a large heatproof bowl, then pour the hot stock over the top. Stir to combine, then cover the bowl with plastic wrap and stand for 5 minutes or until liquid is absorbed. Fluff the couscous with a fork.

- Add the lemon rind and lemon juice to the couscous and mix again with a fork to separate the grains.

- Meanwhile, heat a barbecue hotplate or chargrill pan to medium–high direct heat. Thread the lamb onto the soaked skewers and cook for 2 minutes on each side, or until done to your liking. Remove to a plate, cover and keep warm.

- Increase the heat to high, then barbecue or chargrill the zucchini slices for 2 minutes on each side, or until just cooked. Remove the zucchini from the heat, roughly chop, then stir it through the couscous with the onion and coriander. Season to taste.

- Spoon the couscous onto serving plates. Top with the lamb skewers, sprinkle with extra coriander and serve.

Meat

LAMB 'SAUSAGES' WITH ZUCCHINI AND PEA RISONI

preparation time 20 minutes
cooking time 15 minutes
serves 4

2 tablespoons olive oil
1 onion, finely chopped
1 garlic clove, crushed
1 teaspoon dried oregano
400 g (14 oz) minced (ground) lamb
1 egg, lightly beaten
2 tablespoons chopped flat-leaf
    (Italian) parsley
1 tablespoon chopped mint
2 tablespoons lemon juice

MINTED YOGHURT

250 g (9 oz/1 cup) Greek-style
    yoghurt
1–2 tablespoons chopped mint

ZUCCHINI AND PEA RISONI

200 g (7 oz/1 cup) risoni
    (rice-shaped pasta)
3 tablespoons olive oil
155 g (5½ oz/1 cup) frozen peas
3 small zucchini (courgettes),
    finely sliced
10 cherry tomatoes, halved
2 tablespoons chopped flat-leaf
    (Italian) parsley
juice and finely grated rind of 1 lemon
75 g (2½ oz/½ cup) crumbled soft
    feta cheese

• Preheat a barbecue hotplate or non-stick frying pan to medium direct heat and brush with 1 tablespoon of the oil. Add the onion and garlic and cook for 3 minutes, or until the onion has softened. Stir in the oregano, remove from the heat and leave to cool.

• Transfer the onion mixture to a large bowl. Add the lamb, egg, parsley, mint and lemon juice and mix until well combined. Divide the mixture into eight even portions, then form each into a 'sausage' about 10 cm (4 inches) long. Place on a plate, cover with plastic wrap and refrigerate for 10 minutes.

• To make the minted yoghurt, put the yoghurt in a small bowl, mix the mint through, then cover and refrigerate until required.

• Brush the barbecue hotplate or frying pan with the remaining oil, then cook the sausages for 5–6 minutes on each side, or until cooked through and browned all over.

• Meanwhile, make the zucchini and pea risoni. Bring a large saucepan of salted water to the boil, add the risoni and cook according to the packet instructions, then drain well. Heat the olive oil in a large saucepan over medium heat, add the peas, zucchini and tomato and cook for 2 minutes, or until the tomato starts to soften. Stir in the risoni, parsley, lemon juice and lemon rind, then cook for 1 minute to heat through.

• Serve the sausages on a bed of risoni, with a dollop of the yoghurt and a scattering of feta over the top.

LAMB CHOPS WITH SWEET POTATO MASH AND CHERMOULA

preparation time 20 minutes
cooking time 20 minutes
serves 4

3 orange sweet potatoes (about
    1 kg/2 lb 4 oz), peeled and cut into
    2 cm (¾ inch) chunks
50 g (1¾ oz) butter, chopped
3 tablespoons extra virgin
    olive oil, plus extra, for brushing
8 lamb chump chops
2 tablespoons lemon juice
2 teaspoons honey, or to taste
2 large handfuls of baby English
    spinach

CHERMOULA

1 tablespoon sweet paprika
1 tablespoon ground coriander
1 tablespoon ground cumin
3 tablespoons lemon juice
4 garlic cloves, finely chopped
2 tablespoons honey
2 tablespoons olive oil
1 large handful of flat-leaf (Italian)
    parsley, chopped
1 large handful of coriander (cilantro)
    leaves, chopped

● To make the chermoula, put the paprika, ground coriander and cumin, lemon juice, garlic, honey and olive oil in a small bowl. Season to taste with sea salt and freshly ground pepper, mix well and set aside.

● Bring a large saucepan of salted water to the boil. Add the sweet potato and cook over medium heat for 10 minutes, or until soft. Drain well, then place in a food processor with the butter and blend to a smooth purée. Season to taste with sea salt and freshly ground pepper, then transfer to a heatproof bowl. Cover with foil and keep warm.

• Meanwhile, preheat a barbecue hotplate or chargrill pan to medium–high direct heat. Brush lightly with oil, add the chops and cook for 3–4 minutes on each side, or until they are done to your liking.

• In a small bowl, whisk together the lemon juice, olive oil and honey, then season to taste. Divide the spinach leaves among the serving plates and drizzle the dressing over.

• Divide the sweet potato mash and chops among the plates.

• Mix the parsley and coriander into the chermoula and spoon it over the chops and mash.

LAMB BURGER WITH HUMMUS AND BEETROOT

preparation time 20 minutes
cooking time 10 minutes
serves 2

350 g (12 oz) minced (ground) lamb
1 teaspoon ground cinnamon
½ small red onion, finely chopped
1½ tablespoons currants
2 tablespoons chopped mint
3 tablespoons crumbled
    feta cheese
1 garlic clove, crushed
125 g (4½ oz) tin chickpeas
    (garbanzo beans), rinsed and
    drained
1 tablespoon lemon juice
1 tablespoon extra virgin olive oil
1 tablespoon tahini
1 tablespoon vegetable oil
2 x 8 cm (3¼ inch) long pieces
    Turkish bread
1 small handful rocket (arugula)
225 g (8 oz) tin beetroot
    (beets) slices, drained

● Combine the lamb mince, cinnamon, onion, currants, mint, feta and half the garlic in a bowl. Season to taste with sea salt and freshly ground black pepper, then stir to mix well.

● To make the hummus, place the remaining garlic, chickpeas, lemon juice, olive oil and tahini in a food processor and process until a smooth paste forms, adding up to 1 tablespoon of water to moisten, if necessary. Season to taste and set aside.

● Preheat a barbecue hotplate or small heavy-based frying pan to medium–low direct heat. Divide the lamb mixture in half and form each half into a patty about 7 cm (2¾ inches) in diameter. Brush with oil, add the patties and cook for 10 minutes, turning once, or until golden and cooked through.

● Slice the Turkish bread in half horizontally and toast. Top one half with the rocket, a lamb patty, a slice of beetroot and some hummus. Serve immediately.

Meat

HERBED LAMB CUTLETS WITH STEAMED GREENS AND TAPÉNADE

preparation time 20 minutes plus 15–20 minutes refrigeration
cooking time 10 minutes
serves 4

60 g (2¼ oz/1 cup) fresh
  breadcrumbs
2 large handfuls flat-leaf (Italian)
  parsley, finely chopped
3 tablespoons finely chopped
  oregano
plain (all-purpose) flour, for dusting
2 eggs
8 lamb cutlets

50 ml (1½ fl oz) olive oil, plus extra,
  for drizzling
250 g (9 oz) baby green beans, cut in
  half diagonally
140 g (5 oz/1 cup) frozen peas
155 g (5½ oz/1 cup) frozen broad
  (fava) beans
1 tablespoon mint leaves
4 tablespoons ready-made tapénade

● Combine the breadcrumbs, parsley and oregano in a shallow bowl. Place the flour in another shallow bowl and season with sea salt and freshly ground black pepper. Place the egg in a third bowl, add 1 tablespoon cold water and stir to combine well.

● Dip each cutlet into the flour, shaking off any excess, then into the egg mixture and finally into the breadcrumb mixture, lightly pressing to coat well. Place onto a baking paper-lined baking tray and refrigerate for 15–20 minutes to firm the coating.

● Preheat a barbecue hotplate or frying pan to medium–low direct heat and lightly brush with oil. Add the cutlets and cook for 3 minutes each side or until golden and the meat is cooked to your liking. Drain on paper towels to remove excess oil.

• Meanwhile, bring a saucepan of salted water to the boil over medium heat, add the beans and cook for 2 minutes, then add the peas and broad beans and cook for a further minute or until the vegetables are tender. Drain well, then peel the outer shell of the broad beans.

• To serve, place the greens on serving plates, top with the cutlets, scatter with the mint leaves, drizzle with olive oil and serve with the tapénade on the side.

LAMB FILLETS WITH ZUCCHINI FRITTERS AND TAHINI SAUCE

preparation time 15 minutes plus 1 hour standing
cooking time 15 minutes
serves 2

270 g (9½ oz/2 cups) zucchini
  (courgettes), grated
1 egg, lightly beaten
1 brown onion, finely chopped
large pinch ground nutmeg
4 tablespoons plain
  (all-purpose) flour
200 g (7 oz) Greek-style yoghurt
1 teaspoon tahini
1 garlic clove, finely chopped

4 tablespoons vegetable oil
¼ teaspoon ground cumin
½ teaspoon ground paprika
350 g (12 oz) lamb fillets (about
  4 fillets)
200 g (7 oz) cherry tomatoes, halved
handful flat-leaf (Italian) parsley
2 teaspoons olive oil

• Preheat the oven to 150°C (300°F/Gas 2).

• Place the zucchini in a colander, sprinkle lightly with salt, then stand for
1 hour to drain. Squeeze as much liquid as possible from the zucchini and
place in a bowl. Add the egg, onion, nutmeg, flour and 2 teaspoons water,
season to taste with sea salt and freshly ground black pepper and stir to
combine well.

• In another bowl combine the yoghurt, tahini and garlic, season to taste and
refrigerate until required.

• Preheat a barbecue hotplate or frying pan to medium–low direct heat. Brush
with 2 tablespoons of the vegetable oil. When the oil is hot, drop spoonfuls of
the zucchini mixture onto the hotplate, forming 7 cm (2¾ inch) patties about

2 cm (¾ inch) thick. Cook for 8 minutes, turning once, or until golden and cooked through. Transfer to a baking tray lined with paper towels and place in the oven to keep the patties warm.

● Combine the cumin, paprika and ½ teaspoon salt in a small bowl. Heat the hotplate or frying pan to medium. Brush with the remaining oil. Sprinkle the lamb fillets with the spice mix and cook, turning occasionally, for 5 minutes or until golden and just cooked through; the lamb should be pink in the middle.

● Combine the tomatoes, parsley and oil in a bowl. Cut the lamb fillets into pieces and place on serving plates with the tomato salad and the zucchini fritters. Drizzle the fritters with the tahini sauce and serve immediately.

THAI PORK BURGERS WITH NAHM JIM SALAD

preparation time 20 minutes

cooking time 15 minutes

serves 4

1 tablespoon vegetable oil

400 g (14 oz) tin pineapple rings, drained well

2 tablespoons whole-egg mayonnaise

4 hamburger buns, split and toasted

PORK PATTIES

1 small red onion, chopped

2 garlic cloves, finely chopped

1 lemongrass stem, white part only, finely chopped

1 teaspoon grated fresh ginger

600 g (1 lb 5 oz) minced (ground) pork

1 tablespoon fish sauce

1 carrot, grated

1 egg

40 g (1½ oz/½ cup) fresh breadcrumbs

2 tablespoons Thai red curry paste

NAHM JIM SALAD

1 green bird's eye chilli, finely chopped

½ small red onion, finely sliced

1 small handful of Thai basil

1 small handful of mint

1 Lebanese (short) cucumber, finely chopped

1 teaspoon shaved palm sugar (jaggery)

1 tablespoon lime juice

1 tablespoon fish sauce

2 tablespoons kecap manis (available from the Asian section of supermarkets)

- To make the pork patties, put the onion, garlic, lemongrass and ginger in a small food processor or blender and process until a paste forms. Scrape the paste into a bowl and add the pork, fish sauce, carrot, egg, breadcrumbs and Thai curry paste. Season with sea salt and freshly ground black pepper and mix well using your hands.

- Divide the mixture into eight even portions, then shape each into a round patty about 10 cm (4 inches) in diameter.

- Preheat a barbecue hotplate or frying pan to medium direct heat. Brush with oil, then add the patties and cook for 6–7 minutes on each side, or until cooked through. If necessary, heat a second frying pan over medium heat. Add the pineapple rings to the hotplate or second frying pan, in batches if necessary, and cook for 2 minutes on each side, or until lightly browned.

- To make the nahm jim salad, put the chilli, onion, basil, mint and cucumber in a bowl. In a small bowl mix together the palm sugar, lime juice and fish sauce, then pour over the salad and toss to coat.

- Spread the mayonnaise on four of the toasted bun rounds and divide among serving plates.

- Put two patties on each of the bun rounds. Top with the pineapple, then the nahm jim salad. Drizzle with kecap manis, then put the lids on top and serve.

PORK CUTLETS WITH FENNEL PANCETTA STUFFING

preparation time 20 minutes
cooking time about 30 minutes
serves 4

1 kg (2 lb 4 oz) floury potatoes,
   peeled and chopped
40 g (1½ oz) butter
100 ml (3½ fl oz) milk, warmed
2 tablespoons olive oil
6 pancetta slices, about 80 g (2¾ oz)
   in total, finely chopped
1 small fennel bulb, about 200 g
   (7 oz), trimmed and very thinly
   sliced

1 teaspoon thyme
1 slice sourdough bread, torn into
   small pieces
375 ml (13 fl oz/1½ cups) beef stock
4 pork loin cutlets, about 225–250 g
   (8–9 oz) each
1 onion, thinly sliced
1 garlic clove, crushed
4 tablespoons raisins
3 tablespoons white wine

• Place the potatoes in a large saucepan and cover with cold water. Bring to the boil, then reduce the heat and simmer for 10–12 minutes, or until tender. Drain well, then return to the saucepan. Add two-thirds of the butter and all the warm milk and mash until smooth. Season to taste with sea salt and freshly ground black pepper. Cover and keep warm.

• Meanwhile, heat half the olive oil in a small frying pan over medium heat. Add the pancetta, fennel and thyme and sauté for 6–8 minutes, or until the pancetta is golden and the fennel is tender. Remove from the heat. Add the bread pieces and just enough (1–2 tablespoons) of the stock to enable the mixture to hold together. Set aside to cool slightly.

• Create a pocket in each pork cutlet by cutting into one side of each cutlet with a small sharp knife to make a cavity, taking care not to cut through the

sides of the cutlets. Fill each pocket with the cooled pancetta mixture—there may be some leftover.

● Preheat a barbecue chargrill plate to medium direct heat. Brush cutlets with the remaining oil and season well. Cook for 8 minutes on each side, or until the outsides are slightly charred and the meat is cooked through. Remove from the grill, cover with foil and leave to rest in a warm place for a few minutes.

● Meanwhile, heat a frying pan over medium heat and add the remaining butter. Sauté the onion for 5 minutes, add the garlic and cook for 1 minute. Add the raisins, pour in the wine and cook until reduced by half. Add the remaining stock and simmer gently for 5 minutes.

● Serve the cutlets immediately, with the mashed potato and the raisin sauce.

CHARGRILLED CHORIZO AND VEGETABLES WITH ROMESCO SAUCE

preparation time 25 minutes
cooking time 10 minutes
serves 4

6 chorizo sausages, cut on the diagonal into slices 1 cm (½ inch) thick
1 small sweet potato, about 350 g (12 oz), peeled and sliced 1 cm (½ inch) thick
1 eggplant (aubergine), about 450 g (1 lb), thinly sliced
2 yellow capsicums (peppers), cut into 4 cm (1½ inch) chunks
3 zucchini (courgettes), sliced 1.5 cm (⅝ inch) thick
2 red onions, cut into thin wedges
2 tablespoons olive oil
flat-leaf (Italian) parsley sprigs, to garnish

ROMESCO SAUCE
1 red capsicum (pepper), quartered, seeds and membranes removed
2 garlic cloves, unpeeled
1 tomato
3 tablespoons whole blanched almonds
¼ teaspoon Spanish smoked paprika
2 teaspoons red wine vinegar
2 tablespoons extra virgin olive oil
a pinch of chilli flakes (optional)

• Preheat the grill (broiler) to high. To make the romesco sauce, place the capsicum on a baking tray, skin side up, with the garlic and whole tomato. Grill (broil) for 15 minutes, or until the skins are blackened. Allow to cool, then peel and discard the skins from the capsicum, garlic and tomato. Remove the seeds from the tomato. Place the capsicum, garlic and tomato in a food processor with the remaining romesco sauce ingredients and blend until smooth. Season to taste with sea salt and freshly ground black pepper and set aside.

● Preheat a barbecue hotplate or chargrill pan to medium direct heat. Toss the sausages and vegetables in the olive oil and season with sea salt and freshly ground black pepper. Cook the sausages and vegetables for 3–5 minutes on each side, or until all the vegetables are tender and the sausages are cooked.

● Arrange or layer the vegetables and chorizo sausages in a large bowl or on a platter. Drizzle with the romesco sauce, garnish with parsley sprigs and serve.

PORK AND RICOTTA RISSOLES WITH RISONI AND BRAISED FENNEL

preparation time 20 minutes plus 30 minutes refrigeration
cooking time 20 minutes
serves 4

2 tablespoons olive oil
1 onion, finely chopped
2 garlic cloves, crushed
600 g (1 lb 5 oz) minced (ground) pork
185 g (6½ oz/¾ cup) firm, fresh ricotta cheese
1 tablespoon dijon mustard
2 egg yolks
55 g (2 oz/½ cup) dry breadcrumbs
½ teaspoon ground cloves
3 slices of pancetta, finely chopped
1½ tablespoons finely sliced sage

BRAISED FENNEL
2 tablespoons extra virgin olive oil
2 fennel bulbs (about 500 g/ 1 lb 2 oz), cut into thin wedges
250 ml (9 fl oz/1 cup) chicken stock

RISONI
200 g (7 oz/1 cup) risoni (rice-shaped pasta)
80 g (3 oz/½ cup) frozen peas
20 g (¾ oz) butter

● Heat 2 teaspoons of the olive oil in a small frying pan over medium heat. Add the onion and sauté for 3–4 minutes, or until translucent. Add the garlic and cook for a further minute, then set aside to cool.

● Transfer the cooled onion mixture to a bowl and add the pork, ricotta, mustard, egg yolks, breadcrumbs, cloves, pancetta and sage. Season with sea salt and freshly ground black pepper and mix together thoroughly using your hands. Using damp hands, divide each rissole mixture into eight patties. Cover and refrigerate for 30 minutes.

• For the braised fennel, heat the olive oil in a large frying pan over medium heat. Add the fennel and sauté for 5 minutes, or until light golden. Reduce the heat to medium–low and stir in the stock. Cover and simmer for 3–4 minutes, or until the fennel is tender. Season to taste and keep warm.

• Meanwhile, bring a large saucepan of salted water to the boil. Add the risoni and cook for 9 minutes, or until nearly tender. Add the peas and cook for another 2–3 minutes, or until both the risoni and peas are tender. Drain well, then return to the pan with the butter and season to taste. Heat gently to melt the butter, tossing occasionally to coat the risoni. Keep warm.

• Preheat a barbecue hotplate or large non-stick frying pan to medium direct heat and brush with the remaining oil. Cook the rissoles in batches for 3–4 minutes on each side, or until golden and cooked through. Serve immediately, on a bed of risoni with the braised fennel on the side.

Meat

ITALIAN PORK SAUSAGES WITH CURRANT ANCHOVY RELISH

preparation time 20 minutes
cooking time 40 minutes
serves 4

1 eggplant (aubergine), about 400 g
　(14 oz) in total, trimmed and cut
　widthways into 2 cm (¾ inch) slices
4 zucchini (courgettes), cut
　lengthways into slices 1 cm
　(½ inch) thick
olive oil, for brushing
8 thin Italian pork sausages, about
　600 g (1 lb 5 oz) in total
150 g (5½ oz) mixed salad leaves

CURRANT ANCHOVY RELISH

1 tablespoon olive oil
1 onion, finely chopped
1 garlic clove, crushed
4 anchovy fillets, finely chopped
1 teaspoon finely grated orange rind
75 g (2½ oz/½ cup) currants
1 tablespoon red wine vinegar
400 g (14 oz) tin chopped tomatoes
2 tablespoons orange juice
150 g (5 oz) cherry tomatoes

DRESSING

4 tablespoons extra virgin olive oil
2 tablespoons red wine vinegar
1 small garlic clove, crushed
1 teaspoon dijon mustard

- Preheat a covererd barbecue or oven to 200°C (400°F/Gas 6).

- Grease a large baking tray and line with baking paper. Brush the eggplant and zucchini on both sides with olive oil, then arrange on the baking tray in a single layer. Season with sea salt and freshly ground black pepper and roast for 20 minutes. Remove the zucchini from the oven and roast the eggplant for another 10 minutes, or until tender.

- Meanwhile, make the currant anchovy relish.Heat the olive oil in a small saucepan over medium heat. Add the onion and sauté for 6–7 minutes, or until softened. Add the garlic, anchovy and orange rind and cook, stirring, for 1 minute. Add the currants and vinegar. Stir for another minute, then add the tomatoes, orange juice and 125 ml (4 fl oz/½ cup) water. Bring to a simmer, then reduce the heat to low and cook for 15 minutes, or until reduced and slightly thickened. Add the tomatoes and cook for 5 minutes, or until very slightly softened. Remove the relish from the heat and keep warm while you cook the sausages.

- Preheat a barbecue hotplate or frying pan to medium–high direct heat and lightly brush with oil. Add the sausages and cook for 10 minutes, or until well browned and cooked through, turning often.

- Meanwhile, combine all the dressing ingredients in a bowl and whisk well. Season to taste and set aside.

- Toss the roasted eggplant and zucchini with the mixed salad leaves, drizzle the dressing over and toss to combine. Serve with the sausages and currant anchovy relish.

Meat

PORK CHOPS WITH CREAMED CORN AND ASPARAGUS

preparation time 20 minutes
cooking time 35 minutes
serves 8

30 g (1 oz) butter
1 large leek, white part only, rinsed
   well and thinly sliced
2 garlic cloves, crushed
1 tablespoon plain (all-purpose) flour
1 kg (2 lb 4 oz) frozen corn kernels,
   thawed
250 ml (9 fl oz/1 cup) chicken stock
250 ml (9 fl oz/1 cup) cream
4 tablespoons olive oil
3 teaspoons finely grated lemon rind

4 tablespoons sweet paprika
2 teaspoons smoked paprika
8 x 200 g (7 oz) pork loin chops
350 g (12 oz/2 bunches) asparagus
   spears, trimmed

● Melt the butter in a large heavy-based saucepan. Add the leek and garlic and sauté over medium heat for 5 minutes, or until softened.

● Add the flour and cook, stirring, for 1–2 minutes. Add the corn, stock and cream and stir until well combined. Bring to a simmer over low heat, then cook for 20 minutes, stirring occasionally. Remove from the heat.

● Remove 250 g (9 oz/1 cup) of the creamed corn and set aside. Using a food processor or blender, purée the remaining corn mixture until almost smooth, then return to the saucepan. Add the reserved 250 g (9 oz/1 cup) corn mixture and stir to combine and heat through. Keep warm.

● Combine the oil, lemon rind and paprika in a bowl. Add the pork chops and toss to coat, then season with sea salt and freshly ground black pepper.

● Preheat a barbecue hotplate or large frying pan to medium–high direct heat. Cook the pork chops for 2–3 minutes on each side, or until cooked through. Transfer to a plate and cover with foil to keep warm.

● Meanwhile, bring a saucepan of water to the boil over high heat. Add the asparagus and cook for 2 minutes, or until tender. Drain well.

● Divide the pork chops among serving plates. Serve with the creamed corn and asparagus.

PORK SKEWERS WITH PINEAPPLE NOODLE TOSS

preparation time 15 minutes plus 30 minutes marinating
cooking time 10 minutes
serves 4–6

600 g (1 lb 5 oz) pork loin steaks,
 or pork fillet, trimmed and cut into
 2 cm (¾ inch) chunks
1 tablespoon fish sauce
1 garlic clove, crushed
2 teaspoons grated fresh ginger
1 tablespoon soft brown sugar
lime wedges, to serve

PINEAPPLE NOODLE TOSS
150 g (5½ oz) rice vermicelli
1 tablespoon vegetable oil
1 carrot, cut into matchsticks
12 snow peas (mangetout), trimmed
 and sliced lengthways
220 g (8 oz) tin pineapple pieces,
 drained
1½ tablespoons fish sauce
90 g (3 oz/1 cup) bean sprouts,
 tails trimmed
2 tablespoons toasted peanuts,
 chopped
1 bird's eye chilli, sliced
1 small handful of chopped coriander
 (cilantro) leaves
1 tablespoon lime juice
1½ tablespoons fish sauce
1 tablespoon soft brown sugar

- Soak 12 wooden skewers in cold water for 30 minutes to prevent scorching.

- Put the pork in a bowl with the fish sauce, garlic, ginger and sugar. Toss to coat the pork well, then cover and refrigerate for 30 minutes. Drain the pork well, then thread about four pieces onto each skewer.

- Meanwhile, put the noodles in a heatproof bowl and pour enough boiling water over to just cover. Leave to stand for 10 minutes, or until softened. Drain.

- Preheat a barbecue hotplate or frying pan to medium–high direct heat and lightly brush with oil. Cook the pork for 3–4 minutes on each side, or until golden and cooked to your liking. Keep warm.

- Meanwhile, prepare the pineapple noodle toss. Heat the oil in a large frying pan or wok over medium heat. Add the carrot and snow peas and stir-fry for 1 minute, then add the noodles, pineapple and fish sauce and stir-fry for another 1–2 minutes. Toss the bean sprouts, peanuts, chilli, coriander, lime juice, fish sauce and sugar through the noodles and cook for a further minute, or until fragrant.

- Divide the noodle toss among serving plates, top with the pork skewers and serve immediately, with lime wedges.

Meat

PORK SAUSAGES WITH CABBAGE CARAWAY BRAISE

preparation time 15 minutes

cooking time 45 minutes

serves 4

4 tablespoons butter

3 onions, thinly sliced

3 large potatoes, peeled and cut into
    2 cm (¾ inch) pieces

225 g (8 oz/3 cups) shredded
    cabbage

1 bay leaf

750 ml (26 fl oz/3 cups) chicken stock

3–4 tablespoons red wine vinegar

1 tablespoon caraway seeds

2 tablespoons vegetable oil

8 thin pork sausages (about 200 g/
    7 oz each)

dijon mustard and flat-leaf (Italian)
    parsley, to serve

APPLE SAUCE

3 granny smith apples

1 tablespoon lemon juice

2 tablespoons caster (superfine) sugar

• Heat the butter in a saucepan over medium heat, add the onion and cook, stirring occasionally, for 5 minutes or until softened. Add the potato, cabbage, bay leaf, stock and vinegar, then season to taste with sea salt and freshly ground black pepper. Bring the mixture to the boil, cover, then reduce the heat to low and cook for about 25 minutes, or until the potato is tender and the liquid is absorbed. Remove the bay leaf, then stir in the caraway seeds.

● Meanwhile, to make the apple sauce, peel, core and thinly slice the apple. Place in a small saucepan with 2 tablespoons water, the lemon juice and caster sugar. Bring to the boil over medium heat, then reduce to low and cook for 20 minutes or until the apple is very soft. Stir to form a purée.

● Preheat a barbecue hotplate or heavy-based frying pan to medium–high direct heat. Brush with oil, add the sausages and cook, turning often, for 15 minutes or until golden and cooked through.

● Place the cabbage and potato on serving plates, place the sausages alongside and top with the apple sauce. Add a teaspoon of mustard, sprinkle with parsley and serve immediately.

Seafood

Although a little care is needed to protect its delicate flesh, seafood is wonderful when cooked on the barbecue.

FISH TORTILLAS WITH A MANGO AND GREEN CHILLI SALSA

preparation time 15 minutes
cooking time 5 minutes
serves 4

8 soft tortillas
1 tablespoon olive oil
500 g (1 lb 2 oz) firm white fish fillets
(such as cod, snapper or flathead),
cut into strips 2 cm (¾ inch) thick
375 ml (13 fl oz) jar of chunky mild
salsa

MANGO AND GREEN CHILLI
SALSA
1 large ripe mango, chopped
1 large green chilli, seeded and finely
chopped
1 small handful of coriander (cilantro)
leaves, chopped
1 tablespoon finely chopped red
onion
½ teaspoon ground cumin
1 tablespoon olive oil
1 tablespoon lime juice

● Put all the mango salsa ingredients in a small bowl and gently mix together.
Season to taste with sea salt and freshly ground black pepper, then cover and
set aside until required.

● Heat the tortillas according to the packet instructions. Keep warm.

● Meanwhile, preheat a barbecue hotplate or frying pan to medium direct heat. Add the fish and cook for 1 minute on each side, or until the fish is almost cooked through. Add the bottled salsa and gently stir to combine. Heat until the salsa is warmed through.

● Spread the tortillas with the fish mixture, top with the mango salsa, then roll up and serve.

TERIYAKI SALMON WITH PUMPKIN MASH AND SNOW PEA SALAD

preparation time 15 minutes
cooking time 20 minutes
serves 4

3 tablespoons mirin (available
   from the Asian section of
   supermarkets)
2 teaspoons sesame oil
4 tablespoons teriyaki sauce
2 teaspoons sesame seeds, toasted
2 tablespoons vegetable oil
4 x 150 g (5½ oz) salmon fillets, skin
   and any small bones removed

PUMPKIN MASH
750 g (1 lb 10 oz) butternut pumpkin
   (squash), peeled, seeded and cut
   into chunks
25 g (1 oz) butter
3 tablespoons milk
125 g (4½ oz) snow peas
   (mangetout), trimmed
90 g (3 oz/1 cup) bean sprouts,
   tails trimmed
1 spring onion (scallion), sliced on
   the diagonal

- Combine the mirin, sesame oil, teriyaki sauce and sesame seeds in a small bowl. Remove a third of the mixture and reserve for the salad dressing.

- To make the pumpkin mash, steam the pumpkin over a saucepan of boiling salted water for 15–20 minutes, or until tender. Drain the pan, add the pumpkin pieces, butter and milk, season to taste with sea salt and freshly ground black pepper and mash well. Cover and keep warm.

- Meanwhile, preheat a barbecue hotplate or frying pan to medium–high direct heat and brush with oil. Add the salmon, skinned side up, and cook for 2 minutes on each side, or until just cooked through but still a little pink in the middle. Remove from the hotplate and set aside.

- Add the teriyaki mixture to the hotplate and bring to a simmer. Cook for 2–3 minutes, or until reduced to a thick glaze consistency. Return the salmon fillets to the hotplate and gently toss to coat in the glaze.

- Meanwhile, put the snow peas in a heatproof bowl and pour over enough boiling water to cover. Leave to stand for 1 minute, or until just softened, then drain well.

- Thinly slice the snow peas lengthways and toss in a bowl with the bean sprouts and spring onion. Add the reserved teriyaki salad dressing and toss to coat.

- Divide the mash among warmed plates and top each with a piece of salmon. Serve with the snow pea salad to the side.

FISH WITH OLIVE OIL MASH AND CRISP PANCETTA

preparation time 15 minutes
cooking time 25 minutes
serves 4

1 kg (2 lb 4 oz) desiree potatoes, or
    floury potatoes, peeled and
    chopped
4 tablespoons extra virgin
    olive oil
1 large garlic clove, thinly sliced
2 teaspoons marjoram, plus extra
    small leaves, to garnish

3 thin pancetta slices, about 50 g
    (2 oz) in total
4 x 180 g (6 oz) blue eye trevalla
    fillets, or other firm white fish fillets
200 g (7 oz) green beans, trimmed
50 g (1¾ oz/½ cup) shaved parmesan
lemon cheeks, to serve

- Bring a saucepan of salted water to the boil. Add the potatoes and cook for 13–15 minutes, or until very tender. Drain well, then return to the pan. Cook over low heat for 2–3 minutes to dry the potatoes, shaking the pan occasionally.

- When the potatoes are nearly cooked, heat 2 tablespoons of the olive oil in a frying pan over low heat. Add the garlic and fry gently for 2–3 minutes, or until starting to turn golden. Add the marjoram and cook for a further 20 seconds.

- Mash the potatoes while they are still hot, then add the garlic oil mixture to the mash and fold through. Cover to keep warm.

- Meanwhile, preheat the grill (broiler) to high. Lay the pancetta on a baking tray and grill (broil) for 2–3 minutes, or until just crisp.

- Season the fish fillets with sea salt and freshly ground black pepper. Preheat a barbecue hotplate or large frying pan to high direct heat. Brush with the remaining oil, add the fish, then cover and cook for 2–3 minutes on each side, or until golden and just cooked through.

● Meanwhile, blanch the beans in a saucepan of boiling water for 2 minutes, then refresh under cold running water. Drain well.

● Mix the parmesan through the mash, then spoon onto serving plates. Top each with a fish fillet. Crumble the pancetta over the top, scatter with small marjoram leaves and serve with the beans and lemon cheeks.

Seafood

DUKKAH-CRUSTED FISH WITH CAULIFLOWER PURÉE

preparation time 15 minutes
cooking time 25 minutes
serves 4

3 tablespoons extra virgin olive oil
40 g (1½ oz) butter
1 small onion, finely chopped
1 garlic clove, finely chopped
500 g (1 lb 2 oz) cauliflower (about
   1 small one), trimmed and cut into
   florets
250 ml (9 fl oz/1 cup) chicken stock
50 ml (2 fl oz) lemon juice

2 eggs
50 ml (2 fl oz) milk
4 x 200 g (7 oz) basa, or other white
   fish, fillets
100 g (3½ oz/¾ cup) dukkah
3 tablespoons vegetable oil
rocket (arugula) and lemon cheeks,
   to serve

• Preheat the oven to 160°C (315°F/Gas 2–3). Heat the olive oil and butter in a saucepan over medium–low heat. Add the onion and garlic and cook for 2–3 minutes or until softened. Add the chopped cauliflower and chicken stock, bring to the boil, then reduce heat to low. Cook, stirring occasionally, for 15 minutes or until most of the liquid has evaporated and the cauliflower is very tender; do not allow cauliflower to brown. Transfer the mixture to a food processor, add lemon juice and process until a smooth purée forms. Season to taste with sea salt and freshly ground black pepper. Transfer to a heatproof bowl, cover tightly with foil and keep warm in the oven.

• Break the eggs into a small bowl and whisk together with the milk.

• Place the dukkah into another small bowl. Dip each piece of fish into the egg mix, drain off excess egg, then coat in the dukkah, pressing dukkah onto fish to coat evenly.

• Preheat a barbecue hotplate or large frying pan to medium direct heat and brush with the vegetable oil. Add the fish and cook for 2–3 minutes on each side or until golden and cooked through.

• Spoon cauliflower purée onto warmed plates and top each with a piece of fish. Serve immediately with lemon cheeks and rocket on the side.

GRILLED SWORDFISH WITH ONION JAM AND WINE POTATOES

preparation time 30 minutes
cooking time 40 minutes
serves 4

500 g (1 lb 2 oz) new, or other small,
    boiling potatoes (about 10)
500 ml (17 fl oz/2 cups) shiraz or
    other fruity red wine
20 g (¾ oz) butter
4 x 200 g (7 oz) swordfish fillets
3 tablespoons olive oil
1 fennel bulb, trimmed and very thinly
    sliced
1 small red onion, finely sliced
1 tablespoon capers, drained
1 small handful flat-leaf (Italian)
    parsley, chopped
2 teaspoons lemon juice, or to taste

ONION JAM
1 large red onion, thinly sliced
50 ml (2 fl oz) lemon juice
½ teaspoon fennel seeds
1 teaspoon brown mustard seeds
    (optional)
2 tablespoons extra virgin olive oil
2 tablespoons caster (superfine) sugar
1 teaspoon finely grated lemon rind

• To make the onion jam, combine the onion and lemon juice in a small stainless-steel saucepan and stand for 5 minutes. Heat a small, heavy-based frying pan to medium–low, add the fennel seeds and mustard seeds, if using, and toast, shaking the pan occasionally, for 1–2 minutes or until just fragrant. Add the seeds, oil and sugar to the onion in the pan, bring to the boil over medium heat, then reduce heat to low and cook for 15 minutes or until the onion has softened and the mixture has thickened. Cool, then stir in lemon rind.

• Meanwhile, combine the potatoes in a saucepan with the wine and 250 ml (9 fl oz/1 cup) water, then bring to the boil. Cook over medium heat for 15 minutes or until the potatoes are tender, then drain. Return the potatoes to the saucepan and crush slightly using the back of a wooden spoon. Add the butter, cover and keep warm.

• Preheat a barbecue hotplate or a large, heavy-based frying pan to medium direct heat. Brush the fish on both sides with half of the oil and season to taste with sea salt and freshly ground black pepper. Place the fish, skin side down, on plate or in pan and cook for 2–3 minutes. Turn and cook for another 2–3 minutes or until just cooked through and remove from the heat. The fish should still be a little pink in the middle.

• In a small bowl combine the fennel, onion, capers and parsley and toss with the lemon juice and remaining oil. Season to taste. To serve, divide the fish and potatoes among warmed plates, top fish with a teaspoon of onion jam and serve with the fennel salad.

TUNA SKEWERS WITH MOROCCAN SPICES AND CHERMOULA

preparation time 20 minutes
cooking time 5 minutes
serves 4

800 g (1 lb 12 oz) tuna steaks
2 tablespoons olive oil
½ teaspoon ground cumin
2 teaspoons finely grated lemon zest

CHERMOULA
½ teaspoon ground coriander
3 teaspoons ground cumin
2 teaspoons paprika
pinch cayenne pepper
4 garlic cloves, crushed
15 g (½ oz) chopped flat-leaf (Italian) parsley
25 g (¾ oz) chopped coriander (cilantro) leaves
4 tablespoons lemon juice
125 ml (4 fl oz/½ cup) olive oil

• Soak 12 wooden skewers in cold water for 30 minutes to prevent scorching.

• Cut the tuna into 3 cm (1 ¼ inch) cubes and put in a shallow non-metallic dish. Combine the oil, cumin and lemon zest and pour over the tuna. Toss to coat, then cover and marinate in the refrigerator for 10 minutes.

• Meanwhile, to make the chermoula, put the ground coriander, cumin, paprika and cayenne pepper in a small frying pan and cook over medium heat for 30 seconds, or until fragrant. Combine with the remaining chermoula ingredients and set aside.

• Preheat a barbecue hotplate or chargrill pan to medium direct heat and lightly brush with oil. Thread the tuna onto the skewers. Cook the skewers for 1 minute on each side for rare or 2 minutes for medium. Serve the skewers on a bed of couscous with the chermoula drizzled over the tuna.

Seafood

CRISP-SKIN BLUE EYE TREVALLA WITH POTATOES AND RED COLESLAW

preparation time 15 minutes
cooking time 15 minutes
serves 4

1 teaspoon wholegrain mustard
1 tablespoon mayonnaise
1 tablespoon sour cream
1 tablespoon orange juice
1 tablespoon red wine vinegar
200 g (7 oz/2⅔ cups) finely shredded red cabbage
4 small beetroots (beets), peeled and grated

3 red onions, peeled and thinly sliced
2 large handfuls chopped parsley
4 tablespoons olive oil
12 new potatoes, very thinly sliced
4 x 160 g (5¾ oz) blue eye trevalla fillets, skin on

• To make the coleslaw, place the mustard, mayonnaise, sour cream, orange juice and vinegar in a small bowl and whisk to combine well. Combine the cabbage, beetroot, onion and parsley in a bowl. Add the dressing, season to taste with sea salt and freshly ground black pepper and toss to combine well.

• Preheat a barbecue hotplate or frying pan to medium–high direct heat and brush with oil. Add the potato slices and cook in a single layer for 5 minutes on each side or until crisp. Remove to paper towels to drain excess oil.

• Reduce the heat to medium. Place the fish, skin side down, on the hotplate, then cook for 4 minutes or until the skin is golden. Turn, season well, then cook for another 3 minutes or until the fish is cooked through. Serve the fish with the coleslaw and crisp potatoes.

TANDOORI FISH CUTLETS

preparation time 15 minutes plus overnight marinating
cooking time 10 minutes
serves 4

4 firm white fish cutlets, such as
    blue-eye, snapper or perch
3 tablespoons lemon juice
1 onion, finely chopped
2 garlic cloves, crushed
1 tablespoon grated fresh ginger
1 red chilli
1 tablespoon garam masala

1 teaspoon paprika
500 g (1 lb 2 oz/2 cups) Greek-style
    yoghurt, plus extra to serve
few drops red food colouring
    (optional)
baby English spinach leaves, to serve
lime wedges, to serve

● Pat the fish cutlets dry with paper towels and arrange in a shallow non-metallic dish. Drizzle the lemon juice over the fish and turn to coat the cutlets with the juice.

● Blend the onion, garlic, ginger, chilli, garam masala, paprika and salt in a blender until smooth. Transfer to a bowl and stir in the yoghurt and the food colouring if using. Spoon the marinade over the fish and turn the fish to coat thoroughly. Cover and refrigerate overnight.

● Preheat a barbecue hotplate to medium direct heat. Remove the cutlets from the marinade and allow any excess to drip off. Cook the cutlets on the barbecue, or under a grill (broiler), for 3–4 minutes each side, or until the fish flakes easily when tested with a fork. Serve with extra yoghurt, baby spinach leaves and lime wedges.

BARBECUED FISH WITH ONIONS AND GINGER

preparation time 15 minutes plus 20 minutes refrigeration
cooking time 20 minutes
serves 4–6

1 kg (2 lb 4 oz) small whole firm white fish, cleaned, gutted and scaled
2 teaspoons bottled green peppercorns, drained and finely crushed
2 teaspoons chopped red chilli
3 teaspoons fish sauce
3 tablespoons oil
2 onions, thinly sliced
4 cm (1½ inch) piece fresh ginger, thinly sliced
3 garlic cloves, cut into very thin slivers
2 teaspoons sugar
4 spring onions (scallions), finely shredded

LEMON AND GARLIC DIPPING SAUCE

3 tablespoons lemon juice
2 tablespoons fish sauce
1 tablespoon sugar
2 small red chillies, finely chopped
3 garlic cloves, chopped

- Wash the fish and pat dry inside and out. Cut two or three diagonal slashes into the thickest part on both sides. In a food processor, process the peppercorns, chilli and fish sauce to a paste and brush over the fish. Refrigerate for 20 minutes.

- Preheat a barbecue hotplate or grill (broiler) to very hot direct heat and then brush with 1 tablespoon of the oil. Cook the fish for 8 minutes each side, or until the flesh flakes easily. If grilling (broiling), don't cook too close to the heat.

- While the fish is cooking, heat the remaining oil in a frying pan and stir the onion over medium heat until golden. Add the ginger, garlic and sugar and cook for 3 minutes. Serve over the fish. Sprinkle with spring onion.

- Stir all the dipping sauce ingredients in a bowl until the sugar has dissolved. Serve with the fish.

THAI FISH CAKES WITH TOMATO SALAD

preparation time 15 minutes plus 30 minutes refrigeration
cooking time 10 minutes
serves 4

600 g (1 lb 5 oz) red fish or flathead
    fillets, skin removed
3 egg yolks
1 tablespoon Thai red curry paste
1 tablespoon sweet chilli sauce
1 tablespoon fish sauce
3 kaffir lime leaves, finely shredded
8 green beans, very thinly sliced
4 tablespoons chopped coriander
    (cilantro) leaves
4 tablespoon peanut oil
steamed jasmine rice and lime
    wedges, to serve

TOMATO SALAD

3 handfuls coriander (cilantro) leaves
3 handfuls mint
2 Lebanese (short) cucumbers, halved
    lengthways, seeds removed and
    sliced on the diagonal
1 avocado, chopped
20 cherry tomatoes, halved
4 tablespoon crushed unsalted
    roasted peanuts

CHILLI DRESSING

2 tablespoons lime juice
2 tablespoons fish sauce
2 tablespoons sweet chilli sauce

• Place the fish into a food processor and process until smooth, or finely chop
with a very sharp knife. Transfer to a bowl and add the egg yolks, curry paste,
sweet chilli sauce, fish sauce, lime leaves, beans and coriander. Mix until well
combined, then roll heaped tablespoons of the mixture into balls and flatten
each into a disc about 5 cm (2 inches) across. Cover and refrigerate for
30 minutes.

• To make the tomato salad, combine all the ingredients except the peanuts in
a bowl. Sprinkle with the peanuts.

- To make the chilli dressing, combine all the ingredients in a bowl and whisk until well combined.

- Preheat a barbecue hotplate or non-stick frying pan to medium direct heat and brush with oil. Cook the fish cakes for 2–3 minutes on each side or until golden and firm to the touch.

- To serve, arrange the fish cakes on serving plates. Top with the salad and spoon over the dressing. Serve with steamed rice and lime wedges.

SALMON WITH MANGO-AVOCADO SALSA

preparation time 15 minutes
cooking time 20 minutes
serves 4

1 large mango, peeled, seeded and
    cut into 1 cm (½ inch) pieces, or
    240 g (8½ oz) tinned mango,
    drained
1 avocado, cut into 1 cm (½ inch)
    pieces
4 spring onions (scallions), thinly
    sliced
    on the diagonal
1 red capsicum (pepper), seeded and
    cut into 5 mm (¼ inch) pieces
250 ml (9 fl oz/1 cup) lime juice

110 g (4 oz/½ cup) caster (superfine)
    sugar
4 tablespoons sweet chilli sauce
    (optional)
4 tablespoons coriander (cilantro)
    leaves
4 tablespoons plain (all-purpose) flour
2 teaspoons paprika
4 x 200 g (7 oz) salmon fillets
600 g (1 lb oz) sweet potato (about
    2 medium), peeled and cut into
    1 cm (½ inch) rounds
250 ml (9 fl oz/1 cup) olive oil

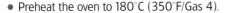

• Preheat the oven to 180°C (350°F/Gas 4).

• Combine the mango, avocado, spring onion and capsicum in a bowl and set
aside. In a saucepan combine the lime juice and sugar and cook over a
medium heat for 3–5 minutes or until mixture boils, reduces and thickens
slightly. Cool, then pour over the mango mixture and set aside. Add the sweet
chilli sauce, if using, and coriander and season to taste with sea salt and freshly
ground black pepper.

• Combine the flour and paprika on a plate, season to taste and mix well. Dust
the salmon in the mixture, shaking off any excess, and set aside. Dust the sweet
potato in the flour and shake off any excess.

● Preheat a barbecue hotplate or frying pan to medium direct heat and brush with 1 tablespoon of the oil. Add the sweet potato slices and cook for 4 minutes on each side or until golden, then drain on paper towels. Wipe the hotplate clean and brush with the remaining oil. Place the salmon on the hotplate, skin side down, and cook for 3 minutes or until the skin is crisp. Turn and cook for 2 minutes or until the salmon is cooked through but still a little pink in the middle.

● To serve, place the sweet potato rounds on serving plates, top with the salmon, spoon over the mango salsa and serve immediately.

SWORDFISH WITH TOMATO BUTTER

preparation time 15 minutes plus 30 minutes marinating
cooking time 10 minutes
serves 4

TOMATO BUTTER

100 g (4 oz) butter, softened
4 tablespoons finely chopped
   semi-dried (sun-blushed) tomatoes
2 tablespoons baby capers in brine,
   drained and crushed
1½ tablespoons shredded basil leaves
4 garlic cloves, crushed
3 tablespoons extra virgin olive oil
300 g (11 oz) slender asparagus
   spears, trimmed
swordfish steaks

● Put the butter in a bowl with the tomato, capers, basil and 2 cloves of crushed garlic, and mash it all together. Shape the flavoured butter into a log, then wrap it in baking paper and twist the ends to close them off. Refrigerate the butter until firm, then cut it into 1 cm ($\frac{1}{2}$ inch) slices and leave it, covered, at room temperature until ready to use.

● Mix 2 tablespoons of the oil and the remaining garlic in a small bowl. Toss the asparagus spears with the oil until they are well coated, season them with salt and pepper, and leave for 30 minutes.

● Preheat a barbecue ridged grill plate to high direct heat. Brush the swordfish steaks with the remaining oil and cook them for 2–3 minutes on each side or until they are just cooked through. Don't overcook the fish as residual heat will continue to cook the meat after it has been removed from the barbecue. Put a piece of the tomato butter on top of each steak as soon as it comes off the barbecue and season to taste. Cook the asparagus on the chargrill plate, turning it regularly, for 2–3 minutes, or until it is just tender. Serve the asparagus immediately with the fish.

Seafood

TUNA BURGER WITH HERBED MAYONNAISE

preparation time 15 minutes
cooking time 10 minutes
serves 4

4 garlic cloves, crushed

2 egg yolks

250 ml (9 fl oz/1 cup) light olive oil

3 tablespoons chopped flat-leaf
  (Italian) parsley

1 tablespoon chopped dill

2 teaspoons dijon mustard

1 tablespoon lemon juice

1 tablespoon red wine vinegar

1 tablespoon baby capers in brine,
  drained

4 anchovy fillets in oil, drained

4 x 150 g (5 oz) tuna steaks

2 tablespoons olive oil

2 red onions, thinly sliced

4 large round bread rolls, halved and
  buttered

100 g (4 oz) mixed lettuce leaves

• Put the garlic and egg yolks in the bowl of a food processor and process
them together for 10 seconds. With the motor running, add the oil in a thin,
slow stream and when the mixture starts to thicken start adding the oil a little
faster. Keep going until all of the oil has been added and the mixture is thick
and creamy, then add the parsley, dill, mustard, lemon juice, vinegar, capers and
anchovies, and process until smooth. Cover and refrigerate the mayonnaise
until you need it.

• Preheat a chargrill plate to high direct heat. Brush the tuna steaks with
1 tablespoon of the olive oil and cook for 2 minutes on each side, or until they
are almost cooked through.

• Add the remaining oil to the onion, toss to separate and coat the rings, and
cook on the flat plate for 2 minutes, or until the onion is soft and caramelized.

• Toast the bread rolls, buttered side down, on the chargrill plate for 1 minute, or until they are marked and golden.

• Put some lettuce, a tuna steak, some of the onion and a dollop of herbed mayonnaise on one half of each roll. Season with salt and pepper, top with the other half of the roll and then serve immediately.

ℕotes *Any left-over mayonnaise will keep for1 week in an airtight container in the refrigerator. Try tossing it through thickly sliced, steamed potatoes for a delicious snack.*

PAPRIKA FISH WITH WARM POTATO SALAD

preparation time 15 minutes
cooking time 15 minutes
serves 4

4 potatoes, peeled and cut into
   2 cm (¾ inch) pieces
4 tablespoons mayonnaise
1 tablespoon light sour cream
2 teaspoons dijon mustard
4 spring onions (scallions), sliced
1 tablespoon capers, chopped
4 garlic cloves, crushed
4 tablespoons coriander (cilantro)
   leaves, chopped

1 tablespoon ground fennel seed
1 tablespoon ground paprika
2 teaspoons finely grated lemon rind
2 tablespoons plain (all-purpose) flour
4 x 200 g (7 oz) basa fillets
125 ml (4 fl oz/½ cup) tablespoons
   extra virgin olive oil
1 tablespoon balsamic vinegar
1 small handful baby spinach leaves
lemon cheek, to serve

● Cook the potato in boiling, salted water for about 8 minutes or until just tender, then drain well. Cool the potato. Combine the mayonnaise, sour cream, mustard, spring onion, capers, garlic and coriander in a bowl. Add the potato and stir gently to combine well.

● Preheat a barbecue hotplate or frying pan to medium direct heat. Combine the fennel, paprika, lemon rind and plain flour. Season to taste. Dust the fish in the flour mixture, shaking off any excess. Heat 2 tablespoons of the oil on the hotplate, add the fish and cook for 2–3 minutes on each side, or until the fish is cooked through and golden brown.

● Meanwhile, combine the balsamic vinegar and the remaining oil in a small jar or bowl and season to taste. Place the fish, potato salad and spinach leaves on a serving plate with the lemon cheek. Serve with the dressing on the side.

SEARED SALMON BITES

preparation time 20 minutes
cooking time 15 minutes
serves 4–6

600 g (1 lb 5 oz) salmon fillet
1 tablespoon cracked black pepper
1 teaspoon sea salt
2 tablespoons olive oil

SPICY COCKTAIL SAUCE

185 g (6½ oz/¾ cup) whole-egg
    mayonnaise
3 tablespoons tomato sauce
2 teaspoons worcestershire sauce
1 teaspoon lemon juice
1 teaspoon sweet chilli sauce
2 teaspoons chopped flat-leaf (Italian)
    parsley

• To make the sauce, stir together the mayonnaise, tomato sauce,
worcestershire sauce, lemon juice, sweet chilli sauce and parsley in a bowl.

• Remove the skin and bones from the salmon fillet and cut into 3 cm
(1¼ inch) cubes and toss the cubes in the combined black pepper and sea salt.

• Preheat a barbecue hotplate or large frying pan to high direct heat and brush
with the oil. Cook the salmon briefly until cooked but still pink in the middle.
Insert a toothpick in each piece and serve with the cocktail sauce.

Seafood

SNAPPER ENVELOPE WITH GINGER

preparation time 20 minutes
cooking time 20 minutes
serves 4

DRESSING
1 spring onion (scallion)
1 small handful coriander (cilantro)
   leaves
1 teaspoon finely grated ginger
2 tablespoons lime juice
1 tablespoon fish sauce
½ teaspoon sesame oil

1 whole snapper (about 1.8–2 kg/
   4 lb–4 lb 8 oz)
sea salt
1 lime
4 spring onions (scallions)
2 large handfuls coriander (cilantro)
   leaves
1 tablespoon finely grated ginger
canola oil spray, for cooking

● To make the dressing, finely slice the green part of the spring onion and the coriander leaves, and mix them together with the ginger, lime juice, fish sauce and sesame oil.

● Check that the fish has been thoroughly scaled, then wash it under cold running water and dry with paper towels. In the thickest part of the flesh make diagonal cuts 1.5 cm (⅝ inch) apart in one direction, then in the other direction, so that the flesh is scored in a diamond pattern. Lightly season the fish with sea salt and freshly ground black pepper.

● Peel the lime, removing all the pith, with a small, sharp knife and separate the lime sections by carefully cutting each piece away from the membrane. Slice the spring onions on the diagonal, mix them with the coriander leaves, lime segments and ginger, and stuff the mixture into the cavity of the fish.

• Lightly spray a double layer of foil with canola oil, making sure it is large enough to wrap around the fish and totally enclose it. Fold the foil around the fish and seal the edges tightly.

• Preheat a kettle or covered barbecue to medium indirect heat. Put the fish in the middle of the barbecue and cook it, covered, for 10 minutes. Use a large metal spatula to turn the fish and cook it for another 8–10 minutes, or until it flakes when tested in the thickest part of the flesh.

• When the fish is cooked, open the foil and slide it onto a plate. Pour the cooking juices over the fish, drizzle the dressing over the top and serve straight away. It is delicious with steamed jasmine rice and a green salad.

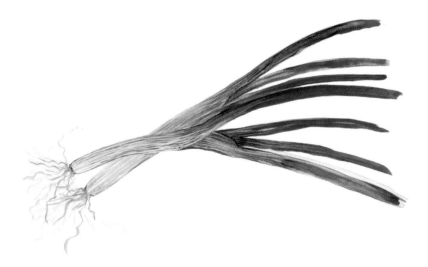

ROSEMARY TUNA KEBABS

preparation time 20 minutes
cooking time 20 minutes
serves 4

3 tomatoes
1 tablespoon olive oil
2–3 small red chillies, seeded and
   chopped
3–4 garlic cloves, crushed
1 red onion, finely chopped
3 tablespoons dry white wine or
   water
600 g (1 lb 5 oz) tinned chickpeas,
   rinsed and drained
3 tablespoons chopped oregano
4 tablespoons chopped flat-leaf
   (Italian) parsley
lemon wedges, to serve

TUNA KEBABS

1 kg (2 lb 4 oz) tuna fillet, cut into
   4 cm (1½ inch) cubes
8 rosemary stalks, about 20 cm
   (8 inches) long, with leaves
olive oil, for brushing

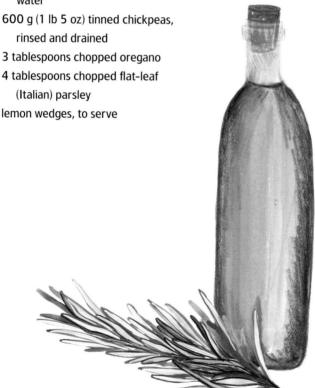

• Cut the tomatoes into halves or quarters and scoop out the seeds. Roughly chop the flesh.

• Heat the oil in a large non-stick frying pan. Add the chilli, garlic and red onion and stir over medium heat for 5 minutes, or until softened. Add the chopped tomato and the white wine or water. Cook over low heat for 10 minutes, or until the mixture is soft and pulpy and most of the liquid has evaporated.

• Stir in the chickpeas with the oregano and parsley. Season to taste.

• Preheat a barbecue hotplate or grill (broiler) to medium direct heat. Thread the tuna onto the rosemary stalks, lightly brush with oil, then cook, turning, for 3 minutes. Do not overcook or the tuna will be dry and fall apart. Serve with the chickpeas and lemon wedges.

Note *Swordfish, striped marlin or salmon are also suitable for this recipe.*

Seafood

DEVILS AND ANGELS ON HORSEBACK

preparation time 10 minutes
cooking time about 5 minutes
makes 24

4–6 bacon slices
12 pitted prunes
12 oysters, fresh or bottled
2 tablespoons worcestershire sauce
Tabasco sauce, to taste

• Soak 24 toothpicks in cold water for
30 minutes to prevent them scorching.
Cut each bacon slice into thin strips.

• Wrap a piece of bacon around each
prune and secure with a skewer.

• Remove the oysters from their shells,
or drain from the bottling liquid. Sprinkle
lightly with worcestershire sauce and ground black pepper, to taste. Wrap each
oyster in bacon, securing with a toothpick.

• Preheat a lightly greased barbecue flatplate or grill (broiler) to medium direct
heat. Cook the savouries, turning occasionally, until the bacon is crisp. Serve
sprinkled with a dash of Tabasco sauce.

HERBED SCALLOP KEBABS

preparation time 1 hour
cooking time 10 minutes
makes 24

24 cleaned scallops (without roe)
6 large spring onions (scallions), green
    part only
2 zucchini (courgettes)
2 carrots

20 g (¾ oz) butter, melted
2 teaspoons lemon juice
1 tablespoon dry white wine
2 teaspoons mixed dried herbs
½ teaspoon onion powder

• Soak 24 wooden skewers in cold water for 30 minutes to prevent scorching.

• Wash the scallops, slice or pull off any vein, membrane or hard white muscle, then pat dry with paper towels. Cut the spring onions in half lengthways, then into 8 cm (3 inch) lengths. Line a baking tray with foil.

• Using a vegetable peeler, slice the zucchini and carrots lengthways into thin ribbons. Plunge the vegetable strips into a bowl of boiling water, leave for 1 minute, then drain. Plunge into a bowl of iced water and leave until cold. Drain and pat dry with paper towels.

• Roll each scallop in a strip of the spring onion, carrot and zucchini and secure with a wooden skewer.

• Preheat a barbecue hotplate or grill (broiler) to medium direct heat. Combine the butter, lemon juice and wine in a small bowl. Brush over the scallops. Sprinkle with the combined herbs and onion powder. Cook for 5–10 minutes, or until the scallops are tender and cooked through.

Note Scallops can be prepared several hours ahead. Refrigerate, covered, until needed.

Seafood

BARBECUED SEAFOOD PLATTER

preparation time 40 minutes
cooking time 30 minutes
serves 6

6 Balmain bugs or slipper lobsters
30 g (1 oz) butter, melted
1 tablespoon oil
12 black mussels
12 scallops on their shells
12 oysters
18 raw large prawns (shrimp), unpeeled

SALSA VERDE

1 tablespoon chopped preserved lemon
20 g (¾ oz/1 cup) flat-leaf (Italian) parsley 1 tablespoon drained bottled capers
1 tablespoon lemon juice
3 tablespoons oil

VINEGAR AND SHALLOT DRESSING

3 tablespoons white wine vinegar
4 French shallots, finely chopped
1 tablespoon chopped chervil

PICKLED GINGER AND WASABI SAUCE

1 teaspoon soy sauce
3 tablespoons mirin
2 tablespoons rice wine vinegar
¼ teaspoon wasabi paste
2 tablespoons finely sliced pickled ginger

SWEET BALSAMIC DRESSING

1 tablespoon olive oil
1 tablespoon honey
125 ml (4 fl oz/½ cup) balsamic vinegar

THAI CORIANDER SAUCE

125 ml (4 fl oz/½ cup) sweet chilli sauce
1 tablespoon lime juice
2 tablespoons chopped coriander (cilantro)

- Freeze the bugs for 1 hour to immobilize. Cut each bug in half with a sharp knife, then brush the flesh with the combined butter and oil. Set aside while you prepare the rest of the seafood.

- Scrub the mussels with a stiff brush and pull out the hairy beards. Discard any broken mussels, or open ones that don't close when tapped on the bench.

- Pull off any vein, membrane or hard white muscle from the scallops, leaving any roe attached. Brush the scallops with the combined butter and oil. Cook them, shell side down, on the barbecue.

- Remove the oysters from the shells, then rinse the shells under cold water. Pat the shells dry and return the oysters to their shells. Cover and refrigerate all the seafood while you make the dressings.

- To make the salsa verde, combine all the ingredients in a food processor and process in short bursts until chopped. Transfer to a bowl and add enough oil to moisten the mixture. Season. Serve a dollop on each scallop.

- To make the vinegar and shallot dressing, whisk the vinegar, shallot and chervil in a bowl until combined. Pour over the cooked mussels.

- To make the pickled ginger and wasabi sauce, whisk all the ingredients in a bowl until combined. Spoon over the cooked oysters.

- To make the sweet balsamic dressing, heat the oil in a pan, add the honey and vinegar and bring to the boil, then boil until reduced by half. Drizzle over the cooked bugs.

- To make the Thai coriander sauce, combine all the ingredients in a jug or bowl and drizzle over the cooked prawns.

- Preheat a barbecue hotplate to medium direct heat. Cook the seafood: the mussels, scallops, oysters and prawns all take 2–5 minutes to cook. The bugs are cooked when the flesh turns white and starts to come away from the shell.

Seafood

CHILLI PRAWN SKEWERS

preparation time 15 minutes
cooking time 5 minutes
makes 30

30 large raw prawns (shrimp)
60 g (2 oz) butter
1 garlic clove, crushed
2 teaspoons soft brown sugar
2 tablespoons lemon or lime juice
2 tablespoons finely chopped
    coriander (cilantro) sprigs
2 tablespoons finely chopped basil
    leaves
1 tablespoon sweet chilli sauce

• Peel the prawns, leaving the tails intact. Gently pull out the dark vein from each prawn back, starting from the head end.

• Preheat a barbecue hotplate to medium direct heat. Add the butter until melted, then add the garlic, sugar, juice, coriander, basil and sweet chilli sauce. Mix thoroughly, add the prawns, then cook over medium heat for 5 minutes, or until the prawns turn pink and are cooked through.

• Thread each prawn onto a bamboo skewer or strong toothpick to serve.

Note Prepare the prawns several hours ahead. Cook just before serving. Scallops or oysters can be used instead of prawns, or alternate pieces of fish with prawns.

SCALLOP AND FISH ROSEMARY SKEWERS

preparation time 10 minutes
cooking time 15 minutes
serves 4

2 tablespoons marjoram leaves

1 tablespoon lemon juice

4 tablespoons olive oil, plus extra, for brushing

3 tablespoons chopped flat-leaf (Italian) parsley

8 long firm rosemary branches

50 g (2 oz) rocket (arugula) leaves

600 g (1 lb 5 oz) firm white fish fillets, cut into 3 cm (1¼ inch) cubes

16 scallops with roe attached

2 heads radicchio, green outer leaves removed, cut into 8 wedges

lemon wedges

● Pound the marjoram leaves in a mortar and pestle with a little salt, or very finely chop them until they become a paste. Add the lemon juice, then stir in the olive oil and parsley, and season to taste.

● Pull the leaves off the rosemary branches, leaving just a tuft at the end of each stem. Thread three pieces of fish and two scallops alternately onto each rosemary skewer, brush them with a little olive oil and season well.

● Preheat a barbecue hotplate to medium direct heat. Cook the skewers for 3-4 minutes on each side or until the fish is cooked through. While the skewers are cooking, add the radicchio to the plate in batches for 1-2 minutes on each side or until it is just wilted and slightly browned. Put the radicchio wedges on a tray in a single layer so that the leaves don't steam in their own heat.

● Arrange the radicchio on a flat serving dish, gently combine with the rocket and drizzle a little marjoram dressing across the top. Serve the skewers with the radicchio salad, lemon wedges and the extra dressing.

Seafood

BARBECUED OCTOPUS

preparation time 20 minutes plus overnight marinating
cooking time 5 minutes
serves 6

170 ml (5½ fl oz/⅔ cup) olive oil
10 g (¼ oz) chopped oregano
3 tablespoons chopped flat-leaf
   (Italian) parsley
1 tablespoon lemon juice

3 small red chillies, seeded and finely
   chopped
3 garlic cloves, crushed
1 kg (2 lb 4 oz) baby octopus
lime wedges, to serve

- To make the marinade, combine the oil, herbs, lemon juice, chilli and garlic in a large bowl and mix well.

- Use a small, sharp knife to remove the octopus heads. Grasp the bodies and push the beaks out from the centre with your index finger, then remove and discard. Slit the heads and remove the gut. If the octopus are too large, cut them into smaller portions.

- Mix the octopus with the herb marinade. Cover and refrigerate for several hours, or overnight.

- Preheat a barbecue hotplate or chargrill pan to high direct heat Drain and reserve the marinade from the octopus. Lightly oil the barbecue. Cook the octopus for 3–5 minutes, or until the flesh turns white. Turn frequently and brush generously with the marinade during cooking.

BARBECUED ASIAN-STYLE PRAWNS

preparation time 15 minutes
cooking time 5 minutes
serves 4

500 g (1 lb 2 oz) large raw prawns
   (shrimp)
lime wedges, to serve

MARINADE
2 tablespoons lemon juice
2 tablespoons sesame oil
2 garlic cloves, crushed
2 teaspoons grated fresh ginger

• Peel the prawns, leaving the tails intact. Gently pull out the dark vein from each prawn back, starting from the head end.

• Mix the lemon juice, sesame oil, garlic and ginger in a bowl. Add the prawns and gently stir to coat the prawns. Cover and refrigerate for at least 3 hours.

• Preheat a barbecue hotplate or chargrill pan to high direct heat Lightly oil the barbecue plate, then cook the prawns for 3−5 minutes, or until pink and cooked through. Brush frequently with marinade while cooking. Serve immediately with the lime wedges.

note Alternatively, the prawns can be threaded onto bamboo skewers. Soak the skewers in cold water for about 30 minutes, or until they sink. This will prevent the skewers burning during cooking. After marinating, thread the prawns evenly onto the skewers and cook as stated, turning and basting occasionally during cooking.

Seafood

STUFFED CALAMARI WITH LIME AND CHILLI SAUCE

preparation time 25 minutes
cooking time 10 minutes
serves 4

DIPPING SAUCE
4 tablespoons lime juice
3 tablespoons fish sauce
2 tablespoons grated palm sugar or
   soft brown sugar
1 small red chilli, finely sliced into
   rounds

12 medium squid
12 raw prawns (shrimp), peeled,
   deveined and chopped
150 g (5½ oz) minced (ground) pork
4 garlic cloves, crushed
½ teaspoon finely grated ginger
3 teaspoons fish sauce
2 teaspoons lime juice
1 teaspoon grated palm sugar
2 tablespoons chopped coriander
   (cilantro) leaves
peanut oil, for brushing

• To make the dipping sauce, put the lime juice, fish sauce, palm sugar and chilli in a small bowl and stir it all together until the sugar has dissolved. Cover the bowl and leave it until you are ready to eat.

• Gently pull the tentacles away from the tube of the squid (the intestines should come away at the same time). Remove the quill from inside the body and throw it away, as well as any white membrane. Pull the skin away from the hood under cold running water, then cut the tentacles away from the intestines and give them a good rinse to remove the sucker rings. Finely chop the tentacles and keep them to add to the stuffing.

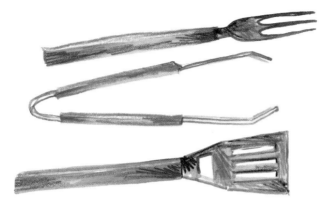

● Put the prawns, pork, garlic, ginger, fish sauce, lime juice, palm sugar, coriander and chopped tentacles in a bowl and mix them together. Use a teaspoon to put some of the stuffing in each tube and push it to the bottom, then secure the hole with a toothpick. Take care to not overfill the tubes as the stuffing will expand when you cook them.

● Preheat a barbecue hotplate or chargrill plate to medium direct heat, brush the squid tubes with peanut oil, and barbecue them for 8 minutes, or until they are cooked through, turning them when the flesh becomes opaque and slightly charred. Remove the tubes from the grill, take out the toothpicks and cut each tube into 1 cm (½ inch) rounds. Serve with the dipping sauce.

Seafood

Salads & vegetables

Don't forget the vegetables for your barbecue – whether as an accompaniment or something more substantial.

CHARGRILLED VIETNAMESE CHICKEN WITH NOODLE SALAD

preparation time 15 minutes
cooking time 15 minutes
serves 6

3 tablespoons lime juice
3 tablespoons fish sauce
1 tablespoon caster (superfine) sugar
1 tablespoon sweet chilli sauce
1 small red onion, thinly sliced
800 g (1 lb 12 oz) chicken thigh
   fillets, trimmed
1 tablespoon peanut oil
80 g (3 oz/½ cup) roasted peanuts

NOODLE SALAD
200 g (7 oz) flat, thin rice noodles
1 carrot, peeled and cut into thin
   matchsticks
1 telegraph (long) cucumber, seeded
   and thinly sliced
65 g (2½ oz/¾ cup) bean sprouts
50 g (2 oz/1 cup) shredded Chinese
   cabbage
1 small handful mint
1 small handful coriander (cilantro)
   leaves
1 small handful basil
1 large red chilli, seeded and thinly
   sliced

• Place the lime juice, fish sauce, caster sugar, sweet chilli and red onion in a small bowl and stir until well combined. Set aside.

• Preheat a barbecue chargrill plate or large chargrill pan to medium direct heat. Place the chicken and oil in a bowl, season to taste with sea salt and freshly ground black pepper and toss to combine well. Cook the chicken for 5 minutes on each side or until cooked through. Remove to a warmed plate, cover loosely with foil and stand in a warm place for 5 minutes. Slice thinly on the diagonal.

● To make the noodle salad, cook the noodles in boiling water for 3 minutes or according to packet instructions until tender, then drain well. Stand under cold running water until cool, then drain well. Place the noodles in a large bowl with the carrot, cucumber, bean sprouts, cabbage, herbs and chilli and toss to combine well.

● Add the chicken and prepared dressing to the noodle salad and gently toss to combine. Divide among serving plates, sprinkle with the peanuts and serve.

Salads & vegetables

SESAME BEEF SALAD WITH AVOCADO AND GRAPEFRUIT

preparation time 10 minutes
cooking time 5 minutes
serves 4

3 ruby grapefruits
600 g (1 lb 5 oz) beef eye fillet
1 tablespoon olive oil
4 large handfuls watercress sprigs or
   rocket (arugula)
2 avocados, sliced
4 tablespoons snipped chives

GINGER DRESSING
2 tablespoons olive oil
2 tablespoons sherry
1 tablespoon white wine vinegar
1 teaspoon sesame oil
1 teaspoon fresh ginger juice
2 tablespoons toasted sesame seeds

● To make the ginger dressing, place all the ingredients in a small bowl and whisk until well combined.

● Using a small sharp knife, peel the grapefruits, taking care to remove all the white pith. Then carefully remove the segments by cutting between the white membrane and flesh. Set aside.

● Preheat a barbecue hotplate or chargrill pan to high direct heat. Brush the beef with oil, then cook for 1 minute on each side for rare, or until cooked to your liking. Remove the beef to a plate and cool to room temperature.

● Divide the watercress sprigs among serving plates. Slice the beef thinly across the grain and arrange on the watercress. Top with the sliced avocado and grapefruit. Sprinkle with the chives. Drizzle the salad with the dressing and serve immediately.

CARAMELIZED ONION AND POTATO SALAD

preparation time 20 minutes
cooking time 50 minutes
serves 10–12

2 tablespoons oil
6 red onions, thinly sliced
1 kg (2 lb 4 oz) kipfler, desiree or
   pontiac potatoes
4 bacon slices
35 g (1 oz/¾ cup) snipped chives

MAYONNAISE
250 g (9 oz/1 cup) whole-egg
   mayonnaise
1 tablespoon dijon mustard
2–3 tablespoons lemon juice
2 tablespoons sour cream

● Heat the oil in a large heavy-based frying pan, add the onion and cook over low–medium heat for 40 minutes, or until caramelized.

● Cut the potatoes into large chunks (if small, leave them whole) and steam or boil for 5–10 minutes until just tender (pierce with the point of a small knife — if the potato comes away easily, it is ready). Drain and cool slightly.

● Remove the rind from the bacon and grill (broil) until crisp. Drain on crumpled paper towels and cool slightly before roughly chopping.

● Put the potato, onion and chives in a large bowl, reserving a few chives for garnish, and toss to combine.

● To make the mayonnaise, whisk the ingredients together in a bowl. Pour over the salad and toss to coat. Sprinkle with the bacon and garnish with the reserved chives.

Salads & vegetables

WARM VEGETABLE AND LENTIL SALAD

preparation time 15 minutes

cooking time 1 hour

serves 4–6

600 g (1 lb 5 oz) kipfler (fingerling) potatoes, scrubbed and halved

600 g (1 lb 5 oz) sweet potatoes, peeled and cut into 3 cm (1¼ inch) chunks

12 French shallots, peeled

350 g (12 oz/1 bunch) baby carrots, trimmed and scrubbed

1 large cauliflower, about 900 g (2 lb), cut into florets

4 tablespoons olive oil

4 rindless bacon slices, about 160 g (6 oz) in total, chopped

400 g (14 oz) tin lentils, rinsed and drained

100 g (3½ oz) baby English spinach leaves

DRESSING

125 ml (4 fl oz/½ cup) chicken stock

125 ml (4 fl oz/½ cup) cream

1½ tablespoons white wine

25 g (1 oz) crumbled blue cheese

3 tablespoons grated parmesan

125 g (4½ oz) chilled butter, chopped

- Preheat the oven to 200°C (400°F/Gas 6). Grease and line two baking trays with baking paper.

- Arrange the potato and sweet potato in a single layer on one of the baking tray, and spread the shallots, carrots and cauliflower on the other. Drizzle each with 1 ½ tablespoons of the olive oil and turn to coat. Season with sea salt and freshly ground black pepper and roast for 50–60 minutes, or until golden and tender; remove the vegetables as they are cooked, as some may require less cooking time than others. Set aside to cool for 10 minutes.

- Meanwhile, heat the remaining oil in a non-stick frying pan over medium heat. Add the bacon and sauté for 6–7 minutes, or until golden. Drain the bacon on kitchen paper, then transfer to a large bowl. Add the lentils, spinach and remaining roasted vegetables and toss gently to combine. Keep warm.

- To make the dressing, pour the stock, cream and wine into a small saucepan and bring to the boil. Reduce the heat to medium–low and simmer for 5–10 minutes, or until reduced by half. Reduce the heat to low, then add the blue cheese and parmesan and stir to combine. Whisking constantly, add the butter a few pieces at a time, making sure it has emulsified into the sauce before adding more. Season to taste. Remove from the heat and cool to room temperature.

- Drizzle some of the dressing over the warm roast vegetable salad and gently toss to combine. Divide the salad among serving plates and serve drizzled with the remaining dressing.

Salads & vegetables

TOMATO AND BOCCONCINI SALAD

preparation time 15 minutes
cooking time Nil
serves 6–8

12 ripe roma (plum) tomatoes
10 bocconcini (fresh baby
     mozzarella cheese)
1 handful basil leaves

DRESSING
125 ml (4 fl oz/½ cup) extra virgin
     olive oil
4 tablespoons balsamic vinegar

● Cut the tomatoes lengthways into 3–4 slices (discard the outside slices, which won't lie flat). Slice each bocconcini lengthways into 3–4 slices. Arrange some tomato slices on a serving plate, place a bocconcini slice on top of each and scatter with some basil leaves. Repeat until all the tomato, bocconcini and basil have been used. Season with salt and pepper.

● To make the dressing, whisk the oil and vinegar together. Drizzle the dressing over the salad.

Note This salad can also be served with a pesto dressing. Finely chop 1 large handful basil leaves, 2 tablespoons pine nuts, 50 g (2 oz/½ cup) grated parmesan cheese and 2 crushed garlic cloves in a food processor. With the motor running, add 125 ml (4 fl oz/½ cup) olive oil and 2 tablespoons lemon juice in a steady stream.

WALDORF SALAD

preparation time 20 minutes
cooking time Nil
serves 4–6

2 green apples, cut into small pieces
2 red apples, cut into small pieces
2 tablespoons lemon juice
4 celery sticks, sliced
3 tablespoons walnut pieces
250 g (9 oz/1 cup) whole-egg
    mayonnaise
chopped flat-leaf (Italian) parsley, to
    garnish (optional)

• Put the apple in a large bowl, drizzle with the lemon juice and toss to coat (this prevents the apples from discolouring). Mix in the celery and most of the walnut pieces.

• Add the mayonnaise to the bowl and toss until well coated. Season to taste. Spoon the salad into a serving bowl, sprinkle with the remaining walnut pieces and serve. Garnish with parsley.

BRAISED BEETROOT SALAD WITH GOAT'S CHEESE CROÛTES

preparation time 35 minutes plus 30 minutes standing

cooking time 45 minutes

serves 4–6

4 beetroot (beets) (about 750 g/
   1 lb 10 oz), with stems and leaves

250 ml (9 fl oz/1 cup) red wine

500 ml (17 fl oz/2 cups) vegetable
   stock

4 tablespoons red wine vinegar

2 tablespoons caster (superfine) sugar

1½ tablespoons olive oil

1 garlic clove, crushed

2 teaspoons oregano, chopped

1 small (25 cm/10 inch) baguette,
   cut into 12 slices, each about
   5 mm (¼ inch) thick

80 g (3 oz/⅔ cup) crumbled goat's
   cheese

3 tablespoons flat-leaf (Italian)
   parsley

RAISIN DRESSING

2 teaspoons soft brown sugar

2 tablespoons red wine vinegar

1 teaspoon dijon mustard

3 tablespoons finely chopped raisins

3 tablespoons extra virgin olive oil

● To make the raisin dressing, place the sugar, vinegar and 125 ml
(4 fl oz/½ cup) water in a small saucepan. Stir over medium heat until the
sugar has dissolved. Add the mustard and raisins and simmer for 5 minutes.
Remove from the heat and leave to stand for 30 minutes. Whisk in the olive oil
and season to taste with sea salt and freshly ground black pepper.

● Trim the beetroot, reserving the stems and leaves. Wash the beetroot bulbs,
then peel and cut them into 2.5 cm (1 inch) wedges and place in a medium
saucepan. Pour in the wine, stock and 2 tablespoons of the vinegar, then stir in
the sugar. Bring to the boil over medium heat, then cover and simmer for
20 minutes.

● Wash and dry the reserved beetroot stems and leaves. Reserving the leaves,
cut the stems into 5 cm (2 inch) lengths, then add to the beetroot wedges in
the pan. Cover and simmer for a further 15 minutes, or until the wedges are
tender. Add the reserved leaves, then cover and cook for a further
4−5 minutes, or until the leaves are tender. Remove from the heat and set
aside to cool. Drain well and transfer to a large bowl.

● Meanwhile, preheat the oven to 180°C (350°F/Gas 4). Combine the olive oil,
garlic and oregano in a small bowl. Brush the mixture over one side of the
baguette slices and arrange on a baking tray. Spread with the goat's cheese and
bake for 5−8 minutes, or until golden and crisp.

● Drizzle the raisin dressing over the beetroot and add the parsley. Toss to
combine and season to taste. Serve with the croutons.

BEAN, MUSHROOM AND MINT SALAD WITH LIME CHILLI DRESSING

preparation time 30 minutes plus overnight soaking
cooking time 35 minutes
serves 6

110 g (4 oz/½ cup) dried split mung
    beans, soaked overnight
2 tablespoons peanut oil
250 g (9 oz) mixed Asian mushrooms
    such as shiitake, shimeji, king and
    enoki, coarsely chopped
90 g (3 oz/1 cup) bean sprouts,
    tails trimmed
2 garlic cloves, finely chopped
5 snake (yard long) beans, cut into
    4 cm (1½ inch) lengths
1 butter lettuce, leaves separated,
    washed and spun dry
1 handful mint leaves
1 handful Thai basil leaves

LIME CHILLI DRESSING
4 tablespoons finely grated palm
    sugar (jaggery)
2 tablespoons lime juice
2 tablespoons light soy sauce
¼ bird's eye chilli, finely diced

PANCAKE BATTER
225 g (8 oz/1¼ cups) rice flour
2 teaspoons ground turmeric
½ teaspoon sea salt flakes
375 ml (13 fl oz/1½ cups) chilled
    sparkling mineral water
270 ml (9½ fl oz) coconut milk
3 spring onions (scallions), thinly
    sliced

- To make the lime chilli dressing, put the palm sugar and 125 ml (4 fl oz/½ cup) water in a small saucepan and stir over medium heat until the sugar has dissolved. Leave to cool, then stir in the lime juice, soy sauce and chilli. Set aside.

- Line a steamer or bamboo basket with muslin (cheesecloth). Drain the soaked mung beans and place in the steamer or bamboo basket. Place over a saucepan of boiling water. Cover and cook for 15 minutes, or until just tender. Remove from the heat and set aside.

- Preheat a barbecue hotplate or large non-stick frying pan to high direct heat and brush with the oil. Add all the mushrooms (except any enoki) and stir-fry for 3 minutes, or until golden brown. Add any enoki mushrooms, along with the bean sprouts, garlic and snake beans. Stir-fry for another minute, then season to taste with sea salt and freshly ground black pepper. Transfer to a bowl and wipe the pan clean.

- To make the pancake batter, combine the rice flour, turmeric and salt in a bowl, then mix in the mineral water, coconut milk and spring onion until smooth.

- Add one-quarter of the pancake mixture to the hotplate and swirl to coat the base. Sprinkle one-quarter of the steamed mung beans and one-quarter of the mushroom mixture over one half of the pancake. Cook for 3 minutes, or until deep golden brown, crisp underneath and just cooked through. Fold the other side of the pancake over the filling, then slip the pancake off the hotplate and cut into four pieces.

- Repeat with the remaining pancake batter and filling to make another three pancakes.

- Divide the lettuce leaves and herbs among serving plates. Top with pancake pieces and serve drizzled with the lime chilli dressing.

Salads & vegetables

CHARGRILLED CAULIFLOWER SALAD WITH TAHINI

preparation time 10 minutes
cooking time 10 minutes
serves 4

TAHINI DRESSING
3 tablespoons tahini
1 garlic clove, crushed
3 tablespoons rice vinegar
1 tablespoon oil
¼ teaspoon sesame oil
1 teaspoon lemon juice

2 teaspoons sesame seeds, toasted
1 tablespoon finely chopped flat-leaf
   (Italian) parsley
½ small garlic clove, finely chopped
½ teaspoon finely grated lemon zest
1 cauliflower (about 1.8 kg/4 lb)
2 tablespoons oil
2 baby cos (romaine) lettuces, washed
   and drained
50 g (2 oz/1⅔ cups) watercress
   leaves, washed and drained

• To make the dressing, whisk the tahini, garlic, rice vinegar, oils, lemon juice
and 1 tablespoon of water together and season.

• Stir the sesame seeds, parsley, garlic and lemon zest together.

• Divide the cauliflower into large florets and cut each floret into 1 cm (½ inch)
thick slices, then brush with oil and season well. Preheat the chargrill plate to
medium direct heat and chargrill the cauliflower pieces for 6–8 minutes, or
until they are cooked and golden on both sides.

• Arrange the cos leaves and watercress on a serving dish and top them with
the chargrilled cauliflower slices. Drizzle the tahini dressing over the cauliflower,
sprinkle it with the sesame seed mixture and serve it while it is still piping hot.

TABOULEH

preparation time 20 minutes plus 2 hours soaking and drying
cooking time Nil
serves 6

130 g (4½ oz/¾ cup) burghul (bulgur)
3 ripe tomatoes
1 telegraph (long) cucumber
4 spring onions (scallions), sliced
120 g (4 oz) flat-leaf (Italian) parsley,
   chopped
2 large handfuls mint, chopped

DRESSING
4 tablespoons lemon juice
3 tablespoons olive oil
1 tablespoon extra virgin olive oil

● Put the burghul in a bowl, cover with 500 ml (17 fl oz/2 cups) water and leave for 1½ hours.

● Cut the tomatoes in half, squeeze to remove any excess seeds and cut into 1 cm (½ inch) cubes. Cut the cucumber in half lengthways, remove the seeds with a teaspoon and cut the flesh into 1 cm (½ inch) cubes.

● To make the dressing, put the lemon juice and 1½ teaspoons salt in a bowl and whisk until well combined. Season well with freshly ground black pepper and slowly whisk in the olive oil and extra virgin olive oil.

● Drain the burghul and squeeze out any excess water. Spread the burghul out on a tea towel (dish towel) or paper towels and leave to dry for about 30 minutes. Put the burghul in a large salad bowl, add the tomato, cucumber, spring onion, parsley and mint, and toss well to combine. Pour the dressing over the salad and toss until evenly coated.

Salads & vegetables

TOMATO SALAD WITH MINT PEPPER DRESSING, RAITA AND POPPADOMS

preparation time 15 minutes
cooking time 5 minutes
serves 4

800 g (1 lb 12 oz) mixed tomatoes,
   such as black Russian, ox heart,
   vine-ripened, grape and cherry
   tomatoes
½ small red onion, very thinly sliced
1 green chilli, thinly sliced
1½ tablespoons peanut oil
1 teaspoon black mustard seeds
1 teaspoon freshly ground black
   pepper
4 garlic cloves, finely chopped
1 tablespoon finely chopped fresh
   ginger
1 tablespoon lime juice

1 tablespoon vegetable oil, plus extra,
   for pan-frying
2 teaspoons soft brown sugar
1 teaspoon sea salt
1 small handful mint leaves
8 cumin-spiced poppadoms

RAITA
1 Lebanese (short) cucumber,
   chopped
200 g (7 oz) Greek-style yoghurt
1 tablespoon chopped coriander
   (cilantro)
juice of ½ lemon
½ teaspoon sugar

• To make the raita, cut the cucumber into quarters lengthways and remove the seeds. Finely chop the cucumber and place in a small bowl with the remaining raita ingredients. Mix well and season to taste with sea salt and freshly ground black pepper. Set aside.

• Cut the tomatoes into slices, halves or quarters, depending on their size. Place in a serving bowl with the onion and chilli.

- Heat the peanut oil in a small frying pan over medium heat. Add the mustard seeds, pepper, garlic and ginger and cook for 1 minute, or until the garlic is light golden. Add the lime juice, vegetable oil, sugar and salt. Mix together well, then remove from the heat.

- Pour the spice mixture over the tomatoes and gently mix to combine. Scatter with the mint.

- Cook the poppadoms following the packet directions.

- Serve the tomato salad with the poppadoms and raita.

THAI TOFU SALAD

preparation time 45 minutes
cooking time 20 minutes
serves 4

3 tablespoons white sticky (glutinous) rice
2½ tablespoons finely grated palm sugar (jaggery)
2½ tablespoons lime juice
2 tablespoons soy sauce
1 tablespoon peanut oil
600 g (1 lb 5 oz) firm tofu, drained well and cut into 2 cm (¾ inch) cubes
5–6 red Asian shallots, peeled and thinly sliced, or 1 small red onion, halved and thinly sliced

1 lemongrass stem, white part only, very thinly sliced
1 teaspoon chilli flakes, or to taste
1 handful mint leaves
1 handful coriander (cilantro) leaves
1 handful Thai basil leaves
6 kaffir lime leaves, very thinly sliced
pineapple chunks, to serve
chopped tomatoes, to serve
steamed jasmine rice, to serve

- Place the rice in a heavy-based frying pan over medium−low heat. Dry-roast for 8−10 minutes, or until light golden and toasted. Remove from the heat and allow to cool, then transfer to an electric spice grinder or small food processor and grind until a coarse powder forms. Set aside.

- In a small bowl, mix together the palm sugar, lime juice and soy sauce, stirring to dissolve the sugar. Set aside.

- Heat the oil in a frying pan over high heat. Add the tofu in batches and fry for 3 minutes, or until golden, turning to brown all over.

- Return all the tofu to the pan and add the shallot, lemongrass and soy sauce mixture. Cook for 1−2 minutes, or until the mixture starts to bubble. Transfer to a large bowl and add the chilli flakes, herbs and lime leaves. Gently toss to combine.

- Divide the salad among serving bowls. Top with some pineapple and tomato as desired. Sprinkle with the toasted rice powder and serve with steamed jasmine rice.

Salads & vegetables

BEAN SALAD

preparation time 30 minutes
cooking time 2 minutes
serves 8–10

250 g (9 oz) green beans, trimmed
400 g (14 oz) tinned chickpeas
425 g (15 oz) tinned red kidney beans
400 g (14 oz) tinned cannellini beans
270 g (9½ oz) tinned corn kernels
3 spring onions (scallions), sliced
1 red capsicum (pepper), finely
   chopped
3 celery sticks, chopped
4–6 bottled gherkins (pickles),
   chopped (optional)
3 tablespoons chopped mint
3 tablespoons chopped flat-leaf
   (Italian) parsley

MUSTARD VINAIGRETTE
125 ml (4 fl oz/½ cup) extra virgin
   olive oil
2 tablespoons white wine vinegar
1 teaspoon sugar
1 tablespoon dijon mustard
1 garlic clove, crushed

● Cut the green beans into short lengths. Bring a small pan of water to the boil and cook the beans for 2 minutes. Drain and rinse, then leave in a bowl of iced water until cold. Drain well.

● Drain and rinse the chickpeas, kidney beans, cannellini beans and corn kernels. Mix them together in a large bowl with the green beans, spring onion, capsicum, celery, gherkin, mint and parsley. Season with salt and freshly ground black pepper.

● To make the vinaigrette, whisk together the oil, white wine vinegar and sugar in a small jug. Season with salt and black pepper. Whisk in the mustard and garlic. Drizzle over the salad and toss gently.

FENNEL, ORANGE AND ALMOND SALAD

preparation time 10 minutes
cooking time 5 minutes
serves 4

2 fennel bulbs, trimmed
3 oranges
100 g (3½ oz) flaked almonds
150 g (5½ oz) creamy blue cheese,
   crumbled
50 g (2 oz) sun-dried (sun-blushed)
   capsicum (pepper), patted dry and
   thinly sliced

DRESSING
4 tablespoons orange juice
1 tablespoon red wine vinegar
1 teaspoon sesame oil

• Thinly slice the fennel bulbs. Peel the oranges, removing all the white pith, and cut into segments. Toast the almonds in a dry frying pan until golden.

• Combine the fennel, orange and almonds in a bowl. Add the crumbled blue cheese and the sun-dried capsicum. Gently toss to combine.

• Make the dressing by combining the orange juice, red wine vinegar and sesame oil. Drizzle over the salad and serve.

Salads & vegetables

CAESAR SALAD

preparation time 25 minutes
cooking time 20 minutes
serves 6

1 small baguette
2 tablespoons olive oil
2 garlic cloves, halved
4 bacon slices (trimmed of fat)
2 cos (romaine) lettuces
10 anchovy fillets, halved lengthways
100 g (3½ oz/1 cup) shaved
    parmesan cheese
parmesan cheese shavings, extra, to
    serve

DRESSING
1 egg yolk
2 garlic cloves, crushed
2 teaspoons dijon mustard
2 anchovy fillets
2 tablespoons white wine vinegar
1 tablespoon worcestershire sauce
185 ml (6 fl oz/¾ cup) olive oil

● Preheat the oven to 180°C (350°F/Gas 4). To make the croutons, cut the baguette into 15 thin slices and brush both sides of each slice with oil. Spread them on a baking tray and bake for 10–15 minutes, or until golden brown. Leave to cool slightly, then rub each side of each slice with the cut edge of a garlic clove. The baked bread can then be broken roughly into pieces or cut into small cubes.

● Cook the bacon under a hot grill (broiler) until crisp. Drain on paper towels until cooled, then break into chunky pieces.

● Tear the lettuce into pieces and put in a large serving bowl with the bacon, anchovies, croutons and parmesan.

● To make the dressing, place the egg yolks, garlic, mustard, anchovies, vinegar and worcestershire sauce in a food processor or blender. Season and process for 20 seconds, or until smooth. With the motor running, add enough oil in a thin stream to make the dressing thick and creamy.

● Drizzle the dressing over the salad and toss very gently until well distributed. Sprinkle the parmesan shavings over the top.

Salads & vegetables

MOROCCAN PUMPKIN ON PISTACHIO COUSCOUS

preparation time 15 minutes
cooking time 50 minutes
serves 4–6

250 ml (9 fl oz/1 cup) vegetable stock

185 g (7 oz/1 cup) instant couscous

20 g (¾ oz) butter

2 garlic cloves, crushed

1 small onion, finely diced

2 tablespoons finely chopped flat-leaf (Italian) parsley

2 tablespoons finely chopped coriander (cilantro) leaves

3 tablespoons roasted, shelled and roughly chopped pistachio nuts

2 tablespoons ras el hanout or Moroccan spice blend (see Note)

250 g (9 oz/1 cup) Greek-style plain yoghurt

1 tablespoon lemon juice

1 tablespoon honey

1 kg (2 lb 4 oz) pumpkin

2 tablespoons olive oil

• Bring the stock to the boil. Place the couscous in a large bowl, then pour the hot stock over the top. Stir to combine, then cover the bowl with plastic wrap and stand for 5 minutes or until the liquid is absorbed. Fluff the couscous with a fork.

• Melt the butter in a small frying pan, add the garlic and onion and cook them over low heat for 5 minutes, or until they are softened. Add the onion mixture to the couscous with the parsley, coriander, pistachio nuts and 2 teaspoons of the spice mix, stir it together and season to taste. Cover the bowl with plastic wrap and keep it warm.

• Put the yoghurt in a small bowl, stir in the lemon juice and honey, and season to taste with salt and freshly ground black pepper.

- Peel the pumpkin, cut it into 2 cm (¾ inch) thick pieces and toss it in a bowl with the oil and the remaining spice mix. Preheat a covered or kettle barbecue to medium direct heat. Grill the pumpkin, covered, for 45 minutes, or until it is golden all over and cooked through. Pile the couscous onto a serving plate, top it with the grilled pumpkin pieces and serve with the yoghurt dressing.

Note *Ras el hanout is a Moroccan spice mix, and is available from gourmet food stores.*

TOMATO AND HALOUMI SKEWERS

preparation time 30 minutes
cooking time 10 minutes
makes about 24

500 g (1 lb 2 oz) haloumi cheese
5 large handfuls basil
150 g (5½ oz) semi-dried (sun-
    blushed) tomatoes
2 tablespoons balsamic vinegar
2 tablespoons extra virgin olive oil
1 teaspoon sea salt

• Soak 24 small skewers in cold water for 30 minutes to prevent them scorching.

• Preheat a barbecue hotplate or chargrill pan to high direct heat. Cut the cheese into 1.5 cm (⅝ inch) pieces. Thread a basil leaf onto a skewer, followed by a piece of haloumi, a semi-dried tomato, another piece of haloumi and another basil leaf. Repeat to use the remaining ingredients.

• Place the skewers on the barbecue hotplate and cook, turning occasionally until the cheese is golden brown, brushing with the combined vinegar and oil while cooking. Sprinkle with the salt and serve hot or warm.

MARINATED BARBECUED VEGETABLES

preparation time 40 minutes plus 1 hour marinating
cooking time 5 minutes
serves 4–6

3 small slender eggplants
   (aubergines)
2 small red capsicums (peppers)
3 zucchini (courgettes)
6 mushrooms

MARINADE
3 tablespoons olive oil
3 tablespoons lemon juice
2 tablespoons shredded basil
1 garlic clove, crushed

- Cut the eggplants into diagonal slices. Place on a baking tray in a single layer, sprinkle with salt and allow to stand for 15 minutes. Rinse thoroughly and pat dry with paper towels. Trim the capsicums, remove the seeds and membrane and cut into long, wide pieces. Cut the zucchinis into diagonal slices. Trim each mushroom stalk so that it is level with the cap. Place all the vegetables in a large, shallow non-metal dish.

- To make the marinade, combine the olive oil, lemon juice, basil and garlic in a bowl. Whisk until well combined. Pour the marinade over the vegetables and stir gently. Store, covered with plastic wrap, in the refrigerator for 1 hour, stirring occasionally to coat the vegetables.

- Preheat a barbecue hotplate or chargrill pan to high direct heat and lightly grease with oil. Place the vegetables on the barbecue and cook over the hottest part of the fire for 2 minutes on each side. Transfer to a serving dish once browned. Brush the vegetables frequently with any remaining marinade while cooking.

Note Vegetables can be marinated for up to 2 hours. Take them out of the refrigerator 15 minutes before cooking. This dish can be served warm or at room temperature.

Salads & vegetables

Snacks

A tasty snack will keep you and your guests happy until the main fare is ready, or you may just want a light bite to tide you over.

LENTIL TAPÉNADE AND ROAST CAPSICUM TOASTS

preparation time 25 minutes
cooking time 40 minutes
serves 6

1 large red capsicum (pepper), trimmed, seeded and cut into quarters

4 tablespoons extra virgin olive oil, plus extra for brushing

12 x 7 mm (³⁄₈ inch) thick slices of day-old baguette, cut on the diagonal

1 x 400 g (14 oz/2 cups) tin brown lentils, rinsed and drained well

2 garlic cloves, chopped

2 tablespoons capers, drained well

1 tablespoon chopped anchovy fillets

100 g (3½ oz/¾ cup) pitted black olives, chopped

2 teaspoons chopped oregano

1 tablespoon lemon juice

150 g (5½ oz/about 3) bocconcini (fresh baby mozzarella cheese), thinly sliced (optional)

1 large handful baby rocket (arugula)

1 small handful mint leaves

- Preheat the oven to 200°C (400°F/Gas 6). Place the capsicum in a roasting pan and drizzle with 1½ tablespoons of the olive oil. Roast for 25–30 minutes or until very soft and slightly charred around the edges. Remove from the dish, reserving any juices, place in a plastic bag and seal. When cool enough to handle, remove the skins and seeds. Cut into 2 cm (¾ inch) wide strips, combine in a bowl with reserved juices and set aside.

- Place the slices of baguette on a baking tray in a single layer and brush lightly with olive oil. Bake for 10–12 minutes or until crisp and light golden, then transfer to a wire rack and cool.

- Combine the remaining olive oil, lentils, garlic, capers, anchovies, olives, oregano and lemon juice in a food processor and process until a coarse purée forms. Season to taste with sea salt and freshly ground black pepper.

- Add the bocconcini, if using, to the capsicum in the bowl and toss to combine well. Place 2 slices of baguette, overlapping, on a plate and top with a quarter of the capsicum mixture. Repeat with the remaining baguette slices and capsicum, then divide the lentil tapénade among plates, spooning it on top of the capsicum. Top with the rocket and mint leaves and serve immediately.

Snacks

RÖSTI WITH SMOKED SALMON AND HONEY-MUSTARD CREAM

preparation time 15 minutes
cooking time 15 minutes
serves 4

800 g (1 lb 12 oz) desiree potatoes
   (about 4)
1 egg, lightly beaten
3 tablespoons vegetable oil
200 g (7 oz) sliced smoked salmon
1 tablespoon chives, cut into 1 cm
   (½ inch) pieces

HONEY-MUSTARD CREAM
60 g (2 oz/¼ cup) sour cream
1 teaspoon wholegrain mustard
1 teaspoon lemon juice
½ teaspoon honey

• To make the honey-mustard cream, combine all the ingredients in a small bowl. Add about 2 teaspoons of water to make a drizzling consistency, then cover and refrigerate until ready to serve.

• Preheat the oven to 120°C (235°F/Gas ½). Peel the potatoes and coarsely grate. Place the grated potato in a clean tea (dish) towel and gently squeeze out any excess moisture. Place into a bowl and combine with the egg. Season to taste with sea salt and freshly ground black pepper.

• Heat the oil in a large frying pan over medium heat. Cook the potato mixture in batches, using 60 ml (2 fl oz/¼ cup) of the mixture for each rösti, flattening out to make rounds about 8 cm (3¼ inches) across. Cook for 5–6 minutes, turning once, or until golden and cooked through. Transfer to a plate, cover loosely with foil and keep warm in the oven while the remaining mixture cooks.

• To serve, top the rösti with salmon slices, drizzle with the honey-mustard cream and sprinkle with chives.

GARLICKY WHITE BEAN BRANDADE

preparation time 5 minutes
cooking time 5 minutes
serves 4

1 teaspoon olive oil
1 small onion, finely chopped
$\frac{1}{2}$ teaspoon finely chopped
    rosemary
1 small garlic clove, chopped
1 x 400 g (14 oz) tin white beans,
    rinsed and drained
2−3 anchovy fillets (depending
    on size), drained

$1\frac{1}{2}$ tablespoons finely grated
    parmesan cheese
1 tablespoon extra virgin olive oil
toasted baguette, to serve

● Heat the olive oil in a small non-stick frying pan over a medium−low heat.
Add the onion and cook, stirring, for 3 minutes or until translucent. Stir in the
rosemary and garlic and cook for 30 seconds.

● Transfer to the bowl of a food processor along with the white beans,
anchovies, parmesan and 2 tablespoons water. Process until almost smooth.
Add the extra virgin olive oil and process again. Season to taste with sea salt
and freshly ground black pepper.

TURKISH TOAST WITH CARROT-CUMIN PURÉE AND CHICKPEA SALAD

preparation time 1 hour plus overnight soaking
cooking time 1 hour 30 minutes
serves 6

140 g (5 oz/^{2}/$_3$ cup) dried chickpeas
   (garbanzo beans)
600 g (1 lb 5 oz) carrots (about 4),
   peeled and coarsely chopped
1 teaspoon sweet paprika
1½ teaspoons ground cumin
1 large handful coriander (cilantro)
   leaves, chopped
4 tablespoons lemon juice
large pinch cayenne pepper, or to
   taste

200 ml (7 fl oz) olive oil
1 medium eggplant (aubergine)
   (about 325 g/11½ oz), trimmed
   and cut into 2 cm (¾ inch) pieces
2 large tomatoes (about 360 g/13 oz)
   trimmed and cut into 2 cm (¾ inch)
   pieces
1 small handful parsley, chopped
1 loaf Turkish bread

- Soak the chickpeas overnight in enough cold water to cover, then drain well. Place the chickpeas in a saucepan and cover with water. Bring to the boil and cook over medium–high heat for about 1½ hours or until tender, adding extra water to keep chickpeas covered as necessary. Drain well.

- Meanwhile, place the carrots in a saucepan and cover with water. Bring to the boil and cook for about 30 minutes or until very soft, then drain well. Transfer to a food processor, add the paprika, 1 teaspoon of the cumin, half the coriander and lemon juice, cayenne pepper and 4 tablespoons of the olive oil. Season to taste with sea salt and freshly ground black pepper, then cool to room temperature.

• Heat 80 ml (2½ fl oz/⅓ cup) of the olive oil in a frying pan over medium heat. Carefully add the eggplant pieces and cook slowly, turning often for 15–20 minutes or until very soft and deep golden, adding a little more oil if necessary. Transfer the mixture to a colander placed over a bowl to drain, reserving the pan juices. Measure 30 ml (1 fl oz) of the reserved pan juices and return them to the frying pan. Heat over low heat, add the remaining cumin and cook for 1 minute or until mixture foams. Add the tomato, season to taste and cook over medium heat, stirring often, for 5 minutes or until softened. Add the eggplant, parsley and the remaining coriander and lemon juice, then stir in the chickpeas.

• Heat the oven to 200°C (400°F/Gas 6). Slice the Turkish bread on the diagonal into thin slices. Brush with the remaining olive oil and place in a single layer on a baking tray. Bake until the bread is golden.

• Serve the carrot purée with toasted Turkish bread and chickpea salad.

CRAB CAKES WITH GINGER AND SESAME LEAF SALAD

preparation time 25 minutes plus 30 minutes refrigeration
cooking time 20 minutes
serves 6

1 tablespoon pickled ginger, thinly sliced

1 tablespoon light soy sauce

2 teaspoons finely grated ginger

3 tablespoons sesame oil

30 ml (1 fl oz) rice wine vinegar

1 teaspoon caster (superfine) sugar

2 teaspoons sesame seeds, lightly toasted

300 g (10½ oz) waxy potatoes such as desiree, peeled and chopped

1 x 510 g (1 lb 2 oz) tin crabmeat, drained

3 spring onions (scallions), trimmed and thinly sliced

3 tablespoons plain (all-purpose) flour

3 eggs, lightly beaten

60 g (2 oz/1 cup) panko crumbs (Japanese breadcrumbs)

250 ml (9 fl oz/1 cup) vegetable oil

2 large handfuls mixed baby salad leaves, to serve

• Combine the pickled ginger, soy sauce, ginger, sesame oil, rice wine vinegar and sugar in a small bowl and whisk to combine. Stir in the sesame seeds, then set aside.

• Place the potatoes in a saucepan and cover with cold water. Bring to the boil and simmer for 7–10 minutes or until tender. Drain well, then mash until smooth. Add the crabmeat and spring onion, season to taste with sea salt and freshly ground black pepper and mix until well combined. Divide the mixture into six even portions, then shape each into a round, 8 cm (3¼ inch) cake. Cover and refrigerate for 15 minutes or until firm.

• Place the flour, eggs and panko crumbs into three separate shallow bowls. Working with one at a time, place a crab cake into the flour, shaking off any excess, then into the egg, draining off excess and then into the crumbs, patting crumbs on firmly to coat. Place the crumbed cakes on a plate lined with baking paper and place in the refrigerator for 15 minutes or until firm.

• Heat the oil in a large, deep frying pan over medium heat. Cook the crab cakes for 4 minutes on each side or until golden.

• Place the salad leaves in a bowl and toss gently with half the dressing. Divide salad evenly among serving plates, top with crab cakes, drizzle over remaining dressing and serve immediately.

PRAWN AND AVOCADO COCKTAIL WITH CHILLI DRESSING

preparation time 15 minutes

cooking time Nil

serves 4

1 large firm, ripe avocado (about
    300 g/10½ oz)
50 ml (1½ fl oz) lemon juice
550 g (1 lb 4 oz) cooked king prawns
    (shrimp), peeled and cleaned or
    250 g (9 oz) cooked prawn
    (shrimp) meat, cut into 1 cm
    (½ inch) slices
1 small roma (plum) tomato (about
    100 g/3½ oz), finely chopped and
    seeds removed
4 large iceberg lettuce leaves,
    trimmed, washed and dried well

CHILLI DRESSING
3 tablespoons whole-egg mayonnaise
1 tablespoon sour cream
2 teaspoons horseradish cream
2 teaspoons lemon juice
1 tablespoon tomato sauce (ketchup)
½ bird's eye chilli, sliced in half, seeds
    removed and finely chopped
1 tablespoon chopped coriander
    (cilantro) leaves

- To make the chilli dressing, place the mayonnaise, sour cream, horseradish cream, lemon juice, tomato sauce, chilli and coriander in a small bowl and mix to combine well. Season to taste with sea salt and freshly ground black pepper.

- Finely chop the avocado and squeeze over 1 tablespoon of the lemon juice and season to taste.

• Add the prawns and tomato to the chilli dressing and mix until combined.
Very finely slice the lettuce leaves and transfer to a bowl. Sprinkle with
remaining lemon juice and season lightly with sea salt.

• To assemble, divide the lettuce among four 310 ml (11 fl oz/1 ¼ cups)
capacity cocktail glasses. Press down gently with a spoon to compact slightly.
Scatter over the avocado, then top with the prawn mixture. Serve immediately.

SPICED LAMB AND YOGHURT IN PITTA BREAD

preparation time 15 minutes
cooking time 10 minutes
serves 4

2 teaspoons ground cumin

2 teaspoons sweet paprika

1 teaspoon dried oregano

4 tablespoons olive oil

4 tablespoons lemon juice

800 g (1 lb 12 oz) lamb back straps
(or 12 lamb fillets)

400 g (14 oz) tin chickpeas (garbanzo
beans), rinsed and drained

3 garlic cloves, crushed

130 g (4½ oz/½ cup) Greek-style
yoghurt

4 tablespoons finely chopped mint

2 teaspoons caster (superfine) sugar

4 pitta breads, warmed through

8 baby cos (romaine) lettuce
leaves, shredded

4 roma (plum) tomatoes, sliced

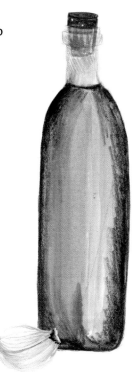

- Combine the cumin, paprika, oregano, 3 tablespoons of the olive oil and 3 tablespoons of the lemon juice in a small shallow bowl. Add the mixture to the lamb, rubbing to coat it, then cover and let stand for 5–10 minutes.

- Meanwhile, combine the chickpeas with the garlic and the remaining oil and lemon juice, and 2 tablespoons of warm water in a food processor and process until a coarse purée forms.

- Place the yoghurt, mint and sugar in a small bowl, mix well to combine, then set aside.

- Preheat a barbecue chargrill or frying pan to high direct heat. Add the lamb and cook for 2–3 minutes each side. Place on a plate and loosely cover with foil for 3 minutes.

- Top the pitta breads with the chickpea purée, shredded lettuce, tomato and sliced lamb. Drizzle with the minted yoghurt and serve immediately, with extra minted yoghurt on the side.

PUMPKIN AND PROSCIUTTO PIZZA WITH HAZELNUT SALAD

preparation time 20 minutes plus 1 hour standing
cooking time 40 minutes
serves 2–4

1 tablespoon olive oil, plus extra,
    for greasing
1 garlic clove, crushed
150 g (5½ oz/1 cup) butternut
    pumpkin, (squash) peeled, seeded
    and cut into 1 cm (½ inch) pieces
3 tablespoons tomato pasta sauce
50 g (1¾ oz) prosciutto (about 4 thin
    slices), torn
100 g (3½ oz) taleggio or mozzarella
    cheese, cut into 5 mm (¼ inch)
    slices
1 small handful mixed salad leaves
1 small handful basil
1 tablespoon hazelnuts, roasted,
    peeled and coarsely chopped
1 teaspoon extra virgin olive oil

PIZZA DOUGH
large pinch caster (superfine) sugar
2 teaspoons active dry yeast
300 g (10½ oz/2 cups) plain
    (all-purpose) flour, plus extra for
    kneading
1½ teaspoon salt
2 tablespoons extra virgin olive oil

- To make the pizza dough, combine 200 ml (7 fl oz) warm water and the sugar in a small bowl, sprinkle over the yeast, then stand in a warm, draught-free place for 7 minutes or until foamy. Combine the flour and salt in a bowl. Add the yeast mixture and oil, then mix until a coarse dough forms. Turn out onto a lightly floured surface and knead for 5 minutes, or until smooth and elastic, adding a little extra flour, if necessary, if dough remains sticky. Lightly oil a bowl, add the dough and turn to coat with oil, then cover the bowl and stand in a draught-free place for 1 hour, or until the dough has doubled in size.

- Preheat the oven to 220°C (425°F/Gas 7). Combine the olive oil, garlic and pumpkin in a roasting pan and bake for 25 minutes or until the pumpkin is cooked through and browned lightly. Remove from the pan and set aside.

- Knock the dough back, then divide into four even pieces. Using a rolling pin, roll each piece of dough out to a round about 18 cm (7 inches) across. Wrap three in plastic wrap, place in an airtight, ziplock bag and freeze for up to 3 weeks, for later use. Place the remaining dough base on a lightly greased baking tray.

- Spread the pasta sauce over the pizza base, then arrange the prosciutto, pumpkin and cheese slices over, leaving a 1 cm (½ inch) border around the edge of the dough. Bake for 12 minutes or until the cheese has melted and the pizza is golden brown.

- Meanwhile, place the salad leaves and basil in a small bowl, add the nuts and oil, then season to taste with sea salt and freshly ground black pepper. Top the hot pizza with the salad and serve immediately.

SMOKED SALMON AND CHARGRILLED VEGETABLE PANZANELLA

preparation time 15 minutes
cooking time 10 minutes
serves 4

4 red onions, halved and cut into
    5 mm (¼ inch) thick wedges
2 red capsicums (peppers), seeded
    and cut into 1.5 cm (⅝ inch) wide
    strips
4 tablespoons extra virgin olive oil
200 g (7 oz) day-old Italian-style
    bread such as ciabatta (about eight
    2 cm/¾ inch wide slices), cut into
    1.5 cm (⅝ inch) pieces
4 very ripe tomatoes, trimmed and
    cut into 1 cm (½ inch) pieces

4 heaped tablespoons pitted green
    olives
3 garlic cloves, crushed
2 tablespoons balsamic vinegar
1 large handful small basil leaves
1 large handful flat-leaf (Italian)
    parsley
4 x 125 g (4½ oz) pieces hot smoked
    salmon or trout, skin and bones
    removed, and coarsely flaked

● Preheat a barbecue hotplate or chargrill pan to medium direct heat. Place
the onion and capsicum pieces in a small bowl with 2 tablespoons of the oil
and toss to combine well. Place the vegetables on the hotplate and cook for
3–4 minutes on each side or until charred and tender. Remove to a plate and
cool. Combine the grilled vegetables, bread, tomato, olives, garlic, vinegar and
the remaining oil in a bowl and toss to combine well.

● Season to taste, then add the remaining ingredients and toss gently to
combine. Pile into a bowl and serve immediately.

POTATO HASH WITH EGG

preparation time 15 minutes
cooking time 15 minutes
serves 4

500 g (1 lb 2 oz) potatoes, such as
    dutch cream or other good
    mashing potato (about 4 small),
    scrubbed
200 g (7 oz) tinned whole baby
    beetroot (beets), drained
200 g (7 oz) cooked corned beef,
    cut into 1 cm (½ inch) pieces

2 onions, very finely chopped
1 large handful flat-leaf (Italian)
    parsley, chopped, plus a few extra
    leaves, to serve
1 tablespoon wholegrain mustard
4 tablespoons olive oil
4 eggs
ready-made tomato chutney, to serve

- Place the potatoes in a saucepan, cover with cold water and bring to the boil over medium heat. Cook for 20 minutes or until tender, then drain well, season with sea salt and coarsely mash.

- Cut the beetroot into 1 cm (½ inch) pieces, then combine with the corned beef, onion, parsley, mustard and potato in a bowl. Season to taste.

- Preheat a barbecue hotplate or non-stick frying pan to medium direct heat. Brush the inside edge of 8 egg-poaching rings with some of the oil. Brush the hotplate with about 3 tablespoons of the oil. Place the rings on the hotplate. Spoon half the potato mixture into the rings and use the back of a spoon to flatten it into the rings. Cook for 6–7 minutes or until browned and crisp on the bottom. Turn over and cook for a further 3–5 minutes or until golden brown.

- Cook the eggs on the barbecue for 3 minutes or until just set. Place 2 hash patties on each serving plate, top with the parsley and remove the egg rings. Add the fried egg and serve immediately with the chutney.

SMOKED CHICKEN WALDORF SALAD ON BRUSCHETTA

preparation time 10 minutes
cooking time 5 minutes
serves 4

4 tablespoons chopped walnuts
    or pecans
8 baguette, ciabatta or sourdough
    bread slices
olive oil, for brushing
1 garlic clove
2 small smoked chicken breasts (each
    about 180 g/6 oz), shredded
1 red apple, cored and cut into 1 cm
    (½ inch) pieces
½ celery stick, cut into 1 cm
    (½ inch) pieces
2 spring onions (scallions), trimmed
    and chopped
100 g (3½ oz) small seedless green
    grapes, halved
2 tablespoons chopped flat-leaf
    (Italian) parsley

DRESSING
4 tablespoons whole-egg mayonnaise
2 teaspoons white wine vinegar
    or lemon juice
2 teaspoons dijon mustard

• To make the dressing, combine all the ingredients in a small bowl, add
1 tablespoon hot water, then whisk until combined. Cover and set aside.

• Toast the walnuts or pecans in a frying pan over a medium–low heat, shaking
the pan often, for 2–3 minutes or until lightly browned. Cool and chop coarsely.

• Preheat the barbecue hotplate or grill (broiler) to medium–high direct heat.
Brush the bread with olive oil, then rub the bread all over with the garlic. Cook
the bread for 1–2 minutes on each side or until lightly golden.

• Combine the chicken, apple, celery, spring onion, grapes, parsley and walnuts
or pecans in a small bowl and stir to mix well. Season to taste with sea salt and
freshly ground black pepper. Add the dressing and toss to combine, then pile
the mixture onto the toasted bread and serve immediately.

Snacks

FRIED EGGPLANT, MOZZARELLA AND BASIL 'SANDWICHES'

preparation time 30 minutes plus 20 minutes standing
cooking time 30 minutes
serves 4

2 eggplants (aubergines), about
    700 g (1 lb 9 oz)
sea salt, for sprinkling
100 g (3½ oz) goat's cheese
100 g (3½ oz/⅔ cup) coarsely grated
    fresh mozzarella cheese
1 tablespoon snipped chives
1 handful basil leaves

75 g (2½ oz/½ cup) plain
    (all-purpose) flour
2 eggs
100 g (3½ oz/1 cup) dry breadcrumbs
2 tablespoons finely chopped flat-leaf
    (Italian) parsley
vegetable oil, for pan-frying
lemon wedges, to serve

● Cut the eggplants into 5 mm (¼ inch) rounds. Spread them on a wire rack and sprinkle with sea salt. Set aside for 20 minutes, or until the eggplant slices are covered in water droplets. Rinse, then pat dry with paper towels.

● Preheat the oven to 120°C (235°F/Gas ½).

● In a small bowl, mix together the goat's cheese, mozzarella, chives and some freshly ground black pepper. Spread the mixture over half the eggplant slices, then top with basil leaves and another eggplant slice of the same size. Press gently to seal.

● Spread the flour on a plate. Whisk the eggs in a wide shallow bowl. Toss the breadcrumbs and parsley together in a bowl and season to taste with sea salt and freshly ground black pepper.

- Dip each eggplant 'sandwich' in the flour, shaking off any excess. Dip into the egg to coat well, then coat evenly with the breadcrumbs.

- In a large non-stick frying pan, heat 1 cm (½ inch) oil over medium–high heat to 180°C (350°F) or until a cube of bread dropped into the oil browns in 15 seconds.

- Working in batches, fry the eggplant sandwiches for 2 minutes on each side, or until golden brown, carefully turning them over with a spatula. Drain on paper towels and keep warm in the oven while cooking the remaining batches.

- Serve immediately, with lemon wedges and some sea salt for sprinkling.

HALOUMI CROÛTES WITH ONION, RAISIN AND OREGANO MARMALADE

preparation time 20 minutes
cooking time 30 minutes
makes 24

1 sourdough baguette, cut into
    24 slices, each about 5 mm
    (¼ inch) thick
olive oil, for brushing and pan-frying
200 g (7 oz) haloumi, cut into
    24 small pieces, each about 5 mm
    (¼ inch) thick
flour, for dusting
oregano, to garnish

ONION, RAISIN AND OREGANO MARMALADE

1½ tablespoons olive oil
2 red onions, thinly sliced
2 teaspoons oregano
3 tablespoons dark brown sugar
2 tablespoons white wine
1 tablespoon balsamic vinegar
4 tablespoons raisins

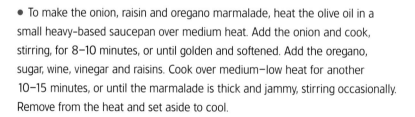

● To make the onion, raisin and oregano marmalade, heat the olive oil in a small heavy-based saucepan over medium heat. Add the onion and cook, stirring, for 8–10 minutes, or until golden and softened. Add the oregano, sugar, wine, vinegar and raisins. Cook over medium–low heat for another 10–15 minutes, or until the marmalade is thick and jammy, stirring occasionally. Remove from the heat and set aside to cool.

● Meanwhile, preheat the oven to 180°C (350°F/Gas 4). Arrange the baguette slices on a large baking tray, in a single layer. Brush with olive oil and bake for 8–10 minutes, or until deep golden and crisp.

● Preheat a barbecue hotplate or large frying pan to medium direct heat and brush generously with oil. Lightly dust the haloumi in flour, shaking off any excess. Cook the haloumi for 1–2 minutes on each side, or until golden. Drain well on paper towels.

● Top each baguette croûte with a piece of haloumi, then some of the marmalade. Garnish with oregano and serve.

Desserts

A sweet little something is always
welcome, no matter how substantial
the barbecued meal has been.

ORANGE-BERRY TRIFLES

preparation time 30 minutes plus 2 hours refrigeration
cooking time Nil
serves 4

375 ml (13 fl oz/1½ cups) custard
250 ml (9 fl oz/1 cup) cream, whipped
1 teaspoon finely grated orange rind
1 tablespoon orange juice
1 tablespoon caster (superfine) sugar
8 savoiardi (lady finger/sponge finger)
    biscuits
4 tablespoons Grand Marnier
    (orange-flavoured liqueur)
    or sherry

155 g (5½ oz/1¼ cups) raspberries
155 g (5½ oz/1 cup) blueberries or
    strawberries, hulled and sliced,
    plus extra, to decorate
4 tablespoons flaked almonds, lightly
    toasted

● Put the custard, whipped cream and orange rind in a large bowl with the orange juice and 2 teaspoons of the sugar. Stir gently to just combine, then cover and refrigerate until required.

● Lay the biscuits out flat, then sprinkle with the liqueur or sherry. Leave for 10–15 minutes, to allow the liquid to be absorbed.

● Put the raspberries and blueberries in a bowl with the remaining sugar and lightly mash with a fork.

● Break each biscuit into three pieces. Take four deep, 375 ml (13 fl oz/ 1½ cups) glasses or bowls and place three biscuit pieces in each. Spoon over half the berry mixture, then half the custard mixture. Repeat the layering with three more biscuit pieces and the remaining berries and custard. Sprinkle with the flaked almonds.

● Cover the trifles with plastic wrap, then put in the refrigerator for at least 2 hours to allow the flavours to develop. Leave the berries at room temperature. Decorate the trifles with more berries just before serving.

RASPBERRY SYLLABUB

preparation time 10 minutes plus 1–2 hours refrigeration
cooking time Nil
serves 4

250 ml (9 fl oz/1 cup) thick
    (double/heavy) cream
2 teaspoons Crème de Cassis
    (blackcurrant-flavoured liqueur)
2 tablespoons caster (superfine) sugar
185 g (6½ oz/1½ cups) fresh or
    thawed frozen raspberries, plus
    extra, to serve
purchased almond bread, to serve

● Combine the cream, Crème de Cassis and half the caster sugar in a bowl. Using electric beaters, whisk the mixture until soft peaks form.

● Combine the remaining sugar and the raspberries in a bowl and mash to a coarse purée with a fork. Gently stir the mashed raspberries into the cream mixture, then divide among four 250 ml (9 fl oz/1 cup) capacity glasses. Cover and refrigerate for 1–2 hours. Top with the extra raspberries and serve immediately, with almond bread on the side.

PASSIONFRUIT YOGHURT ICE CREAM WITH FRUIT

preparation time 30 minutes plus freezing time
cooking time Nil
serves 4

500 g (1 lb 2 oz/2 cups) Greek-style
  yoghurt
125 g (4½ oz/1 cup) icing
  (confectioner's) sugar
125 ml (4 fl oz/½ cup) cream

170 g (6 oz) tin passionfruit pulp in
  syrup
125 g (4½ oz/½ cup) mixed berries
  and chopped fruit, such as kiwi
  fruit and banana

• Combine the yoghurt, icing sugar and cream in a small, freezer-proof container. Add the passionfruit and stir to mix well. Cover the mixture tightly, then freeze for 1 hour or until well chilled. Transfer to an ice-cream machine, churn according to the manufacturer's instructions, then freeze until firm. If you do not have an ice-cream machine, after the 1 hour chilling, beat the yoghurt with electric beaters to break up the ice crystals, then re-freeze for 1 hour. Beat and freeze three more times; then cover and freeze until firm.

• Soften the yoghurt ice cream at room temperature for about 10 minutes before serving. Place 2 scoops in a serving bowl or glass, add the chopped fruit and serve.

CHOCOLATE-DIPPED ICE CREAM BALLS

preparation time 20 minutes plus freezing
cooking time 5 minutes
makes 12

1 litre (35 fl oz/4 cups) vanilla ice
   cream, softened
300 g (10½ oz/2 cups) chopped
   good-quality dark chocolate
1 tablespoon vegetable oil
90 g (3 oz/⅔ cup) chopped pistachio
   nuts

- Line two baking trays with baking paper and freeze until very cold.

- Working quickly, scoop six large balls of ice cream onto each chilled baking tray. Insert an ice cream stick or small cocktail toothpick into each ball. Put the baking trays in the freezer for several hours or overnight, until the ice cream balls are firm.

- Melt the chocolate in a heatproof bowl set over a saucepan of simmering water, ensuring the water does not touch the base of the bowl. Stir the chocolate until smooth. Stir the oil into the chocolate. Allow to cool to room temperature.

- Have the topping prepared as you will need to work quickly. Work with one tray of ice cream balls at a time.

• With the aid of the attached stick and a spoon, dip balls in the chocolate, using the spoon to coat the balls and letting the excess chocolate drip off.

• Immediately sprinkle with the chopped pistachios. Quickly return to the tray and refreeze for 2 hours, or overnight.

ROCKY ROAD ICE CREAM TERRINE

preparation time 20 minutes plus freezing
cooking time 5 minutes
serves 6

180 g (6 oz/¾ cup) chopped glacé cherries

180 g (6 oz/2 cups) marshmallows, chopped

65 g (2 oz/¾ cup) desiccated coconut

100 g (3½ oz) chocolate wafer biscuits, chopped

150 g (5½ oz/1 cup) chopped milk chocolate

2 litres (70 fl oz/8 cups) vanilla ice cream

3 tablespoons chocolate syrup

- Line a 3 litre (104 fl oz/12 cup) loaf (bar) tin with baking paper, allowing a 5 cm (2 inch) overhang at both ends. Place in the freezer for 30 minutes.

- Put the cherries, marshmallows, coconut and wafers in a large bowl and gently mix together.

- Melt the chocolate in a heatproof bowl over a saucepan half-filled with simmering water, ensuring the base of the bowl doesn't touch the water. Stir the melted chocolate through the marshmallow mixture, mixing well to coat the ingredients with the chocolate. Allow to cool to room temperature.

- Meanwhile, remove the ice cream from the freezer for 10 minutes, or until softened slightly. Fold the marshmallow mixture into the softened ice cream and stir to combine well.

- Spoon the ice cream into the loaf tin, smoothing the top even, then freeze for 3 hours or overnight, until firm. To serve, stand the ice cream in the loaf tin at room temperature for 5 minutes to soften slightly before turning out onto a plate. Cut into slices 2 cm (¾ inch) thick and drizzle with chocolate syrup.

YOGHURT, COCONUT AND APRICOT ICE CREAM STICKS

preparation time 15 minutes plus overnight refrigeration and freezing
cooking time Nil
serves 10

1 kg (2 lb 4 oz/4 cups) Greek-style
   yoghurt
30 g (1 oz/$\frac{1}{2}$ cup) flaked almonds,
   lightly toasted
4 tablespoons sultanas (golden
   raisins)
3 tablespoons desiccated coconut

3 tablespoons dried apricots,
   chopped
1 teaspoon natural vanilla extract
175 g (6 oz/$\frac{1}{2}$ cup) honey
2 tablespoons sesame seeds,
   lightly toasted

● Line a large sieve or colander with muslin (cheesecloth), then spoon the yoghurt into the sieve. Stand the sieve over a large bowl. Refrigerate for 6 hours or overnight, or until the yoghurt is well drained and thickened.

● Remove the yoghurt to a large bowl. In a food processor, very finely chop the almonds, sultanas, coconut and apricot, then add to the yoghurt with the remaining ingredients and stir to combine well.

● Divide the mixture among ten 120 ml (3¾ fl oz) ice cream moulds, then insert an ice cream stick into the middle of each one. Freeze for 6–8 hours or overnight, until frozen solid.

● To serve, dip the moulds briefly in a bowl of hot water to loosen the frozen yoghurts. Serve immediately.

Desserts

WHITE CHOCOLATE MOUSSE WITH STRAWBERRIES

preparation time 15 minutes plus 3½ hours refrigeration
cooking time 10 minutes
serves 4

180 g (6 oz/1⅓ cups) chopped
   good-quality white chocolate
300 ml (10½ fl oz) cream
1 teaspoon powdered gelatine
3 eggs, separated
250 g (9 oz) strawberries, hulled
   and sliced

sifted icing (confectioners') sugar,
   for dusting
3 tablespoons Cointreau or other
   orange-flavoured liqueur
1 tablespoon sifted icing
   (confectioners') sugar
1 small handful of mint leaves, torn

• Put the chocolate and cream in a heatproof bowl set over a saucepan of simmering water, ensuring the water does not touch the base of the bowl. Stir until the chocolate has melted and the mixture is smooth, then set aside to cool.

• Pour 1 tablespoon water into a small heatproof cup and sprinkle the gelatine over the top. Leave to stand for 5 minutes, or until the gelatine has softened, then place the cup in a small saucepan of hot water deep enough to come halfway up the side of the cup. Stand over medium–low heat for 3–4 minutes, or until the gelatine has dissolved, ensuring the water in the saucepan doesn't boil. Allow to cool slightly, then stir into the chocolate mixture along with the egg yolks. Refrigerate for 20 minutes, or until thickened slightly.

• Using electric beaters, whisk the egg whites in a dry, clean bowl until firm peaks form. Fold the egg white into the chocolate mixture until evenly combined. Divide among four 250 ml (9 fl oz/1 cup) serving glasses, then cover and refrigerate for 3 hours, or until set.

• Half an hour before serving, macerate the strawberries by tossing the strawberries in a small bowl with the liqueur and icing sugar, then cover and leave to stand for 30 minutes.

• Stir the mint leaves through the macerated strawberries and spoon over the mousse.

LEMON CREPES

preparation time 20 minutes plus 30 minutes refrigeration
cooking time 15 minutes
serves 4

225 g (8 oz/1½ cups) plain
　(all-purpose) flour
2 tablespoons caster (superfine) sugar
3 eggs
500 ml (17 fl oz/2 cups) milk
20 g (¾ oz) melted butter, cooled,
　plus extra butter, for pan-frying

115 g (4 oz/½ cup) ready-made
　lemon curd (lemon butter)
2 tablespoons thick (double/heavy)
　cream
fresh raspberries, to serve

• Sift the flour and a pinch of salt into a bowl, then stir in the sugar and make a well in the centre.

• Whisk the eggs in a small bowl with the milk and melted butter. Pour into the flour mixture and whisk until smooth. Strain the batter into a pouring jug to eliminate any lumps, then cover with plastic wrap and refrigerate for 30 minutes.

• Heat a 22 cm (8½ inch) non-stick frying pan over medium heat. Lightly brush with melted butter, then pour 60 ml (2 fl oz/¼ cup) of the batter into the pan, swirling to coat the pan. Cook for 1 minute, or until the edges are golden, then turn the crepe over and cook for a further minute, or until light golden underneath. Transfer to a warm plate and cover with a paper towel. Repeat with the remaining batter to make 12 crepes, adding a little more butter to the pan as necessary.

• Mix the lemon curd and cream together and spoon into the crepes before folding into quarters. Serve scattered with raspberries.

TROPICAL ETON MESS

preparation time 20 minutes plus 20 minutes cooling
cooking time 30 minutes
serves 4

2 egg whites
115 g (4 oz/½ cup) caster (superfine)
   sugar
500 ml (17 fl oz/2 cups) cream

440 g (15½ oz) tin crushed
   pineapple, drained
170 g (6 oz) tin passionfruit pulp

● Preheat the oven to 140°C (275°F/Gas 1). Line two baking trays with baking paper.

● Using electric beaters, whisk the egg whites in a dry, clean bowl until stiff peaks form. Add the sugar 1 tablespoon at a time, beating well after each addition. Beat until the mixture is thick and glossy and the sugar has dissolved — this should take about 10 minutes.

● Spoon rounded dessertspoonfuls of the mixture onto the baking trays, then bake for 25–30 minutes, or until the meringues are pale and dry. Turn the oven off and leave the meringues in the oven for 20 minutes to cool completely, leaving the door ajar.

● Pour the cream into a large bowl and whip until soft peaks form, using electric beaters.

● Break each meringue into 2.5 cm (1 inch) chunks and place in a large bowl. Spoon the crushed pineapple over, then fold in the whipped cream. Drizzle with two-thirds of the passionfruit pulp and fold gently to create a swirling effect.

● Spoon the mixture into serving bowls, glasses or cups. Drizzle with the remaining passionfruit pulp and serve.

WATERMELON, CRANBERRY AND LIME GRANITA

preparation time 15 minutes plus freezing
cooking time 10 minutes
serves 4

230 g (8 oz/1 cup) caster (superfine)
   sugar
125 ml (4 fl oz/½ cup) cranberry juice
750 ml (26 fl oz/3 cups) fresh
   watermelon juice
3 tablespoons lime juice
125 ml (4 fl oz/½ cup) vanilla vodka

- Place a 2 litre (70 fl oz/8 cup) metal baking tin (or one measuring about 20 x 30 x 4 cm/8 x 12 x 1½ inches) in the freezer to chill.

- Put the sugar in a saucepan with 375 ml (13 fl oz/1½ cups) water. Place over low heat, stirring to dissolve the sugar. Add the cranberry juice, increase the heat to medium–high and bring to the boil. Reduce the heat to low and simmer for 5 minutes. Remove from the heat and leave to cool.

- Stir in the watermelon juice and lime juice, then pour into the baking tin and freeze for 2 hours. Remove from the freezer and stir the mixture with a metal fork to break up the ice crystals, then freeze for another hour, or until firm.

- Before serving, remove the granita from the freezer for 10 minutes to soften slightly. Using a fork, flake the granita into large crystals. Quickly spoon into serving bowls or cups and serve drizzled with the vodka.

Desserts

STRAWBERRY VANILLA ICE CREAM TERRINE

preparation time 40 minutes plus 5 hours freezing
cooking time Nil
serves 6

2 litres (70 fl oz/8 cups) vanilla bean
 ice cream
750 g (1 lb 10 oz/5 cups)
 strawberries, hulled (3 punnets)
2 tablespoons icing (confectioner's)
 sugar

1 tablespoon lemon juice
1 teaspoon rosewater, or to taste
1 small handful small mint leaves

• Line an 11 cm (4¼ inch) deep, 1.875 litre (65 fl oz/7½ cup), 10.5 x 21 cm
(4 x 8¼ inch) loaf (bar) tin with plastic wrap, leaving 5 cm (2 inches)
overhanging on the long sides.

• Divide the ice cream evenly among 2 stainless- steel bowls. Place one of the
bowls back in the freezer, leaving the other to soften slightly.

• Combine 500 g (1 lb 2 oz) of the strawberries in a food processor with
1 tablespoon of the icing sugar and the lemon juice and process until a smooth
purée forms. Pour the strawberry purée through a fine sieve to remove the
seeds, pressing down on the solids to remove as much of the pulp as possible.
Using a large metal spoon mix the strained purée and the softened ice cream
until thoroughly combined, then freeze for 1 hour.

• Remove the vanilla and strawberry ice creams from the freezer. Set aside until starting to soften. Spoon half of the vanilla ice cream into the loaf tin, smoothing the top using the back of the spoon. Top with half of the strawberry ice cream, then repeat with the remaining vanilla and strawberry ice creams. Bring the overhanging plastic wrap over the top of the terrine to cover, then freeze for 4 hours or overnight until firm.

• To serve, quarter the remaining strawberries and place in a bowl with the remaining icing sugar and rosewater. Set aside for 30 minutes, then stir in the mint. Turn the terrine out of the loaf tin and remove the plastic wrap. Slice terrine into 3 cm (1¼ inch) thick slices and serve with the strawberry salad.

Desserts

BUTTERMILK PANNA COTTA WITH CARAMELISED ORANGES

preparation time 30 minutes plus overnight refrigeration
cooking time 15 minutes
serves 6

375 ml (13 fl oz/1½ cups) buttermilk
1 tablespoon powdered gelatine
300 ml (10½ fl oz) cream
125 g (4½ oz) caster (superfine) sugar
½ teaspoon natural vanilla extract

CARAMELISED ORANGES
230 g (8 oz/1 cup) caster (superfine) sugar
3 oranges or 5 blood oranges, peeled and all white pith removed, thinly sliced

● To make the caramelised oranges, put the sugar and 125 ml (4 fl oz/½ cup) boiling water in a saucepan and stir over low heat until the sugar is dissolved. Bring to the boil and cook until the syrup is a deep caramel colour. Remove from the heat. Working quickly and taking care, add 125 ml (4 fl oz/½ cup) water. Swirl the pan, then place over low heat and stir until smooth. Put the orange slices in a large, heatproof bowl and pour syrup over. Allow to cool.

● Place 125 ml (4 fl oz/½ cup) of the buttermilk in a small bowl and sprinkle the gelatine over. Leave until the gelatine softens.

● Place the cream and sugar in a saucepan and while stirring, bring almost to the boil. Add the remaining buttermilk and vanilla and heat again but do not allow to boil. Remove from heat, stand for 5 minutes to cool slightly, then add the gelatine mixture and stir until the gelatine has dissolved. Leave to cool for 10 minutes, then divide the mixture among six 125 ml (4 fl oz/½ cup) capacity moulds that have been rinsed with cold water. Refrigerate overnight. To serve, dip each mould briefly into a bowl of hot water to loosen the panna cotta, then turn out onto plates and serve with caramelised oranges.

TORRIJAS WITH HONEY CREAM

preparation time 10 minutes
cooking time 10 minutes
serves 4

500 ml (17 fl oz/2 cups) milk
4 tablespoons honey
1 teaspoon ground ginger
1 teaspoon natural vanilla extract
8 x 1.5 cm (⅝ inch) thick slices of
    stale baguette, sliced on an angle
160 ml (5¼ fl oz) vegetable oil
3 tablespoons raspberries or other
    berries, to serve
1 tablespoon ground cinnamon
1 tablespoon caster (superfine) sugar

HONEY CREAM
2 tablespoons honey
160 ml (5¼ fl oz) thick (double/heavy)
    cream

- To make the honey cream, combine the honey and cream in a bowl and mix well, then cover and refrigerate until needed.

- Combine the milk, honey, ginger and vanilla in a small saucepan and stir over low heat until the honey is dissolved. Pour into a shallow bowl. Dip the bread slices into the milk mixture, allowing each slice to become quite soaked.

- Heat the oil in a large non-stick frying pan over medium heat. Working in batches if necessary, cook the bread slices for 2 minutes on each side or until golden. Place on serving plates, top with the raspberries, sprinkle with the combined cinnamon and sugar and drizzle with the honey cream. Serve immediately.

Desserts

CHERRY AND ALMOND PARFAIT

preparation time 30 minutes plus 1 hour 10 minutes refrigeration
cooking time 10 minutes
serves 6

600 g (1 lb 5 oz/4 cups) frozen pitted
    cherries, thawed
150 g (5½ oz/⅔ cup) caster
    (superfine) sugar
2 teaspoons cornflour (cornstarch)
250 g (9 oz/1 cup) cream cheese,
    chopped
Finely grated rind of 1 orange

1 teaspoon vanilla extract
300 g (10½ oz) thick (double/heavy)
    cream
2 tablespoons amaretto or other
    almond-flavoured liqueur
    (optional)
75 g (2¾ oz/1½ cups) small almond
    biscotti, coarsely chopped

- Combine the cherries and 115 g (4 oz/½ cup) of the caster sugar in a small saucepan, cover, then slowly bring to the boil. Cook the mixture, stirring occasionally, for 5–6 minutes over medium–low heat or until the cherries have softened and given up their juices.

- Combine the cornflour with 1 tablespoon water in a small bowl and stir until a smooth paste forms. Stirring constantly, add the cornflour mixture to the simmering cherries. Cook, stirring, for 1 minute or until the cherry liquid has boiled and thickened slightly. Remove from the heat and cool to room temperature. Transfer to a bowl, cover, then refrigerate for 1 hour.

• Meanwhile, combine the cream cheese, orange rind, vanilla and the remaining sugar in a bowl and, using electric beaters, beat until mixture is smooth and fluffy. Add the cream and beat for 2–3 minutes or until mixture is thick and smooth, then stir in the amaretto, if using. Transfer the cream to a bowl, cover and refrigerate for 1 hour or until well chilled.

• To assemble the parfait, divide half the cherries among six 250 ml (9 fl oz/ 1 cup) capacity glasses, then spoon half the cream cheese mixture over cherries. Scatter half the biscotti crumbs over cream cheese, then repeat layering, finishing with a layer of crumbs. Serve immediately.

SPICED WINE JELLY

preparation time 30 minutes plus 3 hours refrigeration
cooking time 10 minutes
serves 6

600 ml (21 fl oz) red wine
500 ml (17 fl oz/2 cups) apple and
  blackcurrant juice
220 g (7¾ oz/1 cup) caster
  (superfine) sugar
2 cinnamon sticks

1 teaspoon whole cloves
4 cardamom pods, lightly crushed
3 wide strips orange zest, all white
  pith removed
1½ tablespoons powdered gelatine
vanilla ice cream, to serve (optional)

● Combine the red wine, 400 ml (14 fl oz) of the juice, sugar, spices and zest in
a saucepan and slowly bring nearly to the boil. Remove from the heat, cover
and stand for 30 minutes to allow the flavours to develop, then cool to room
temperature.

● Meanwhile, sprinkle the gelatine over the remaining juice in a small heatproof
bowl and stand for 5 minutes or until the gelatine has softened. Place the bowl
in a small saucepan, add warm water to come halfway up the side of the bowl,
then place over medium–low heat for 5–6 minutes or until the gelatine has
dissolved. Strain the wine mixture, discarding solids, then stir in the gelatine
mixture. Divide among six 200 ml (7 fl oz) moulds, cover and refrigerate
for 3 hours or until firm.

● To serve, dip each jelly mould briefly into a bowl of hot water to loosen jelly,
then turn out onto serving plates or shallow bowls. Serve immediately, with a
scoop of ice cream alongside, if using.

BERRY SAGO PUDDING

preparation time 30 minutes plus 2 hours refrigeration
cooking time 40 minutes
serves 6

750 g (1 lb 10 oz/6 cups) frozen
    mixed berries
65 g (2½ oz/⅓ cup) sago
230 g (8 oz/1 cup) caster (superfine)
    sugar
whipped cream, to serve

● Combine the berries and 125 ml (4 fl oz/½ cup) water in a saucepan, cover and cook over medium heat for 10 minutes or until the berries are soft and have given up all their juices. Strain berries in a colander placed over a bowl, pressing berries gently to extract as much liquid as possible. Reserve solids. Measure the juice, then make the quantity up to 625 ml (21½ fl oz/2½ cups) with water.

● Combine the berry liquid with the sago in a saucepan, then bring to the boil, stirring often, over medium–low heat. Cover, reduce heat to low and cook, stirring often, for 30 minutes or until sago is soft and translucent and mixture has thickened. Take care that mixture does not stick to the base of the pan. Add the sugar, stir until dissolved, then remove from heat. Cool the berry sago to room temperature, then stir in the reserved berry solids. Transfer to a bowl, cover and refrigerate for 2 hours or until chilled. Divide the mixture among serving bowls or glasses, top with whipped cream and serve.

RICE FLOUR PUDDING WITH RHUBARB-ROSEWATER COMPOTE

preparation time 20 minutes plus 30 minutes standing and 1 hour refrigeration
cooking time 20 minutes
serves 4

600 ml (21 fl oz) milk

115 g (4 oz/½ cup) caster (superfine) sugar

1 cinnamon stick

3 cardamom pods, crushed

3 x 1 cm (½ inch) wide strips orange zest

4 tablespoons rice flour

1½ tablespoons cornflour (cornstarch)

chopped pistachios, to serve (optional)

RHUBARB-ROSEWATER COMPOTE

450 g (1 lb) rhubarb (about 1 bunch) trimmed and cut into 1 cm (½ inch) pieces

4 tablespoons orange juice

115 g (4 oz/½ cup) caster (superfine) sugar

½ teaspoon rosewater, or to taste

- To make the rhubarb-rosewater compote, combine rhubarb, orange juice and sugar in a saucepan over medium heat. Cover, bring to the boil, reduce heat to low and cook for 3–4 minutes or until sugar has dissolved and rhubarb has softened. Cool to room temperature, then stir in rosewater. Transfer to a bowl, cover and refrigerate.

- Meanwhile, combine 500 ml (17 fl oz/2 cups) of the milk, sugar, cinnamon, cardamom and orange zest in a saucepan and slowly bring almost to the boil over a low heat, stirring to dissolve sugar. Remove mixture from heat, cover and stand for 30 minutes to allow flavours to infuse. Strain mixture, discarding solids. Combine remaining milk with rice flour and cornflour in a small bowl and stir to form a smooth paste. Reheat the strained milk mixture in a saucepan over medium heat, bring to the boil, then whisking constantly, add the rice flour paste. Cook mixture, whisking constantly, for 5 minutes or until it comes back to the boil. Reduce heat to low and cook, whisking constantly to avoid lumps forming, for 3 minutes or until thick and smooth. Remove from heat and cool slightly, whisking occasionally to prevent lumps or a skin forming. Cool slightly, then divide among four 300 ml (10 $\frac{1}{2}$ fl oz) serving glasses or bowls. Cover and chill for about 1 hour or until set.

- To serve, spoon the rhubarb mixture over the rice puddings, sprinkle with the pistachios, if using, and serve.

Desserts

BANANA SEMIFREDDO WITH RUM-CARAMEL SAUCE

preparation time 30 minutes plus at least 4 hours refrigeration
cooking time 10 minutes
serves 6

3 large egg yolks
125 g (4½ oz/⅔ cup, lightly packed) brown sugar
3 tablespoons dark rum
180 g (6 oz/¾ cup) mashed very ripe banana (about 1)
2 teaspoons lime or lemon juice
200 ml (7 fl oz) cream, whipped
2 large egg whites, at room temperature

RUM-CARAMEL SAUCE
170 g (6 oz/⅔ cup) caster (superfine) sugar
2 tablespoons unsalted butter
2 tablespoons dark rum
125 ml (4 fl oz/½ cup) cream

● Have ready a large bowl with 3 cups of ice and 500 ml (17 fl oz/2 cups) cold water in it. Combine the egg yolks, sugar and rum in a metal bowl. Whisk to combine well, then, whisking continuously, set bowl over a saucepan of boiling water and whisk for 10–12 minutes or until thick and pale. Transfer the bowl to the ice bath and continue whisking until cold.

● Combine the banana and lime juice in a bowl, stirring to mix well, then fold in the whipped cream.

- In a large clean bowl whisk the egg whites and a pinch of salt until firm peaks form. Gently fold the banana mixture into the cooled egg-yolk mixture. Fold a third of the egg whites into the egg-yolk mixture to loosen, then gently fold in the remaining egg white. Divide mixture among six 125 ml (4 fl oz/½ cup) capacity glasses or ceramic ramekins. Cover and freeze for 4 hours or overnight if time permits.

- To make the rum-caramel sauce, combine sugar and 100 ml (3½ fl oz) water in a small heavy-based saucepan over a medium–high heat, stirring until sugar dissolves. Bring to the boil, then reduce heat to low and cook for 5–10 minutes or until caramelised. Remove from the heat and, taking care as mixture will spit, stir in the butter, rum and cream. Return the saucepan to a low heat and stir the sauce continuously until smooth. Cool completely.

- Serve the banana semifreddo topped with the rum-caramel sauce.

GRILLED FIGS WITH HONEYED MASCARPONE

preparation time 5 minutes
cooking time 5 minutes
serves 4

240 g (8½ oz/1 cup) mascarpone
    cheese
1 tablespoon honey
8 figs, cut in half lengthways
4 tablespoons firmly packed brown
    sugar
2 tablespoons toasted flaked almonds

- Preheat the grill (broiler) to medium.

- Combine the mascarpone and honey in a serving bowl.

- Place the figs, skin side down, on a small baking tray, sprinkle with the sugar and grill for 3 minutes or until the sugar is melted and the figs are golden. Transfer to a serving bowl, sprinkle with the almonds and serve immediately with the mascarpone mixture.

STRAWBERRIES WITH RICOTTA CREAM AND MINT

preparation time 10 minutes plus 30 minutes standing
cooking time Nil
serves 4

500 g (1 lb 2 oz) strawberries, hulled and halved

2 tablespoons Cointreau (orange-flavoured liqueur)

60 g (2 oz/½ cup) icing (confectioner's) sugar, sifted

310 g (11 oz/1⅓ cups) ricotta cheese

4 tablespoons thick (double/heavy) cream

4 tablespoons small mint leaves

1 tablespoon toasted pistachio kernels, roughly chopped

• Combine the strawberries, Cointreau and half the icing sugar in a bowl. Toss well to combine, then stand at room temperature for 30 minutes or until the strawberries soften slightly.

• Meanwhile combine the remaining icing sugar, ricotta and cream in a bowl. Toss the strawberries with the mint leaves and transfer to serving glasses, sprinkle with the pistachios and serve immediately with the ricotta cream on the side.

Desserts

Index

Index

Index

Index